P9-CRQ-718

The Little Book of

LEADERSHIP

DEVELOPMENT

50 Ways to Bring Out the Leader in Every Employee

SCOTT J. ALLEN
MITCHELL KUSY

ᴬAMACOM

American Management Association
New York • Atlanta • Brussels • Chicago • Mexico City • San Francisco
Shanghai • Tokyo • Toronto • Washington, D.C.

This publication is designed to provide accurate and authoritative information in regard to the subject matter covered. It is sold with the understanding that the publisher is not engaged in rendering legal, accounting, or other professional service. If legal advice or other expert assistance is required, the services of a competent professional person should be sought.

Library of Congress Cataloging-in-Publication Data

Allen, Scott J., 1972–
    The little book of leadership development : 50 ways to bring out
the leader in every employee / Scott J. Allen, Mitchell Kusy.
        p.   cm.
    Includes bibliographical references and index.
    ISBN-13: 978-0-8144-1754-6
    ISBN-10: 0-8144-1754-X
    1. Leadership.   I. Kusy, Mitchell.   II. Title.

HD57.7.A425   2011
658.4'092—dc22
                                                    2010053493

About AMA
American Management Association (www.amanet.org) is a world leader in talent development, advancing the skills of individuals to drive business success. Our mission is to support the goals of individuals and organizations through a complete range of products and services, including classroom and virtual seminars, webcasts, webinars, podcasts, conferences, corporate and government solutions, business books and research. AMA's approach to improving performance combines experiential learning—learning through doing—with opportunities for ongoing professional growth at every step of one's career journey.

Printing number

10   9   8   7   6   5   4   3   2   1

To four mentors who sparked (and nurtured) my interest in the academic study of human resource development and leadership—Brenda Levya-Gardner, Sharon Korth, Richard Couto, and Jon Wergin.

—Scott J. Allen

To so many who have made this book possible through their generosity, professionalism, and nurturing. Your leadership is something for which I will always be grateful.

—Mitchell Kusy

Contents

Foreword

L EADERSHIP, I HAVE SAID over the years, is the ability to raise one's voice over the general chaotic buzz of an organization and later turn out to have been right. I came up with this "definition" partly out of frustration over all the definitions that there are of this word that attracts so much interest, and partly from a realization that we don't often think of giving or receiving "leadership" in the instant that it is occurring. Only later do we realize that either we or someone else had supplied "leadership."

In the instant we are doing what we think needs doing. Our behavior is specific and concrete, and of course quite complex. Meanwhile, "leadership" is abstract and general. The words we use to talk about it—words about style and about function and about content—similarly tend to be abstract and general. It is very difficult to talk meaningfully about "leadership" in terms of the concrete attitudes and actions leaders display, and in terms of the concrete responses they receive.

There's another problem many of us who teach and consult about leadership continually encounter. If we talk about leadership abstractly, presenting theories and frameworks for thinking about leadership, participants will often object: "This is all too general. How does it apply to my situation?" Whereas if we get down and dirty and try to be as specific as we can about, say, leading a meeting, the response we often get is, "My situation isn't quite like this one you're describing." At this point, if we attempt to elicit the details of a particular participant's situation, we can see the eyes of others beginning to glaze over, because to get really specific about one participant's situation is probably to get into details of personality and of culture and of technology and of formal structure that seem far removed from the situations of other participants.

A final chronic problem with teaching and training about leadership is that there's doing it and then there's talking about it. No amount of talking about it seems to result in people becoming better at doing it. This problem has led to all kinds of attempts to introduce more "experiential" material into classes and training situations. It is very hard to achieve a truly convincing reality to these experiential situations. Adult training and development practices have probably done a better job than the academic environment. We professors keep interrupting experiential material to point out the presence of concepts, or to have people write in journals, or discuss what was going on in the simulation. Such interruptions may be justified for other reasons, but they do detract from the impact of the leadership situations we foster in classrooms. No doubt there are other conundrums associated with teaching and training about leadership. But these three—the split between abstract and concrete, the paradoxes of prescribing generally versus concretely, and the fact that leading and talking about leading are two different things—are enough to make the point: that despite thousands of books and articles about leadership, and who knows how many millions of hours devoted to discussing it, to say nothing of all the actual leading that is going on constantly in the world, the nature of leadership, how to do it better, and how to teach others to do it remain maddeningly elusive. If it weren't so important, we probably should have given up the attempt years ago.

And indeed important it is. As this is being published—at the beginning of 2011—it cannot be more obvious that the world is full of problems that cry out for leadership. We are fond of talking about the leadership that we need from our national and international leaders and from senior executives in organizations, but the fact is that all these individuals can do is inspire more leadership throughout the organizations and institutions that they "lead." New and better things will happen because of the efforts of these more local leaders as much or more than the efforts of the men and women on the world stage.

Against this background, Scott Allen and Mitch Kusy have produced this wonderful little book of practical wisdom about leading and leadership. I welcome their decision not to produce yet another abstract framework that tries to say once and for all what leadership is. Once and for all, there is no "once and for all" about leadership. What exists, though, are lots of ideas about leading more effectively and what the learning process for leadership is. This is what the authors offer. Each of their "tips" pertains to some sort of problem or situation leaders encounter. You can quickly tell that the authors themselves have "been there, done that." Each tip resolves the abstract-versus-concrete issue I mentioned earlier by just staying practical and describing things a leader or leadership educator can actually do to move the learning along.

Are there fifty-one or a hundred and fifty-one such tips that could have gone into this book? Yes, there are as many tips as there are nuances to leadership learning. The point is not whether the authors have captured them all. Rather, each tip will start a reflection process that will lead you on to your own realizations, to your own tips to keep in mind as you go about your leadership learning, regardless of what role you are in.

As a final comment for this Foreword, I want to point out something the authors neglect, and that most writers on management and leadership neglect as a matter of fact. Behind all these tips, and behind everything else that is written about management and leadership, is a general consciousness that focuses on how the organization is working, how the people in it are doing, and what can be done to make the organization more effective and the people in it have a more meaningful and fulfilling experience. We take for granted that this consciousness exists and is understood, but I often wonder if it is. Within all of us is a little bone that wants things to run smoothly and for members to have a good experience without our having to work very hard to achieve it or facilitate it.

In fact, every good leader knows that you have to work on the organization, not just in it, all the time—a distinction I have heard attributed to Peter Drucker. Good leaders also know that the leader-manager's main business is to work on the organization, including on oneself—or better, within oneself and with organization members—to improve the experiences everyone is having. This is the key to productivity; in the long run there is no shortcut whereby people's experience can be ignored or abused in favor of productivity. Allen and Kusy make abundantly clear what this consciousness I speak of entails. Their tips are about these things, emanating from a nonstop and bone-deep concern for how things are working and how people are doing.

—Peter Vaill, Senior Scholar, Antioch University
Ph.D. Program, Leadership and Change

Introduction

M ANY RESEARCH STUDIES suggest that leaders who help team members make sense of their roles in the organization, encourage the development of those around them, stimulate intellectual growth, and model ethical and trustworthy behavior achieve greater results than those who do not. Do you do these things? What would your team say?

The Little Book of Leadership Development is filled with ideas to help you develop leadership capacity in others. This book rests on the notion that *how* you choose to develop others will significantly enhance their technical expertise and their ability to lead others. If you are active, involved, and perceived by members of your team as an individual who cares about their development and growth, you will increase your chances of success and theirs.

By intentionally changing how you lead and manage others, you can develop leadership capacity in those around you every day. If you take time to create a system of leadership development, there will be less need for periodic training and development. It simply will be a function of your department—a thread that weaves throughout the tapestry of your day-to-day operations.

This notion is rooted in the concept that leadership development is not something that primarily occurs in the classroom. It occurs on the job—on the fly—each and every day. Organizations spend billions of dollars on training each year, but often the most valuable resource, the department manager, is left out of the loop. According to leadership scholar Bernard Bass: "Most important to whether training will modify behavior back on the job is the trainee's immediate supervisor."[1] In support of Bass's assertion, many other researchers have found that the level of support and overall attitude of a learner's boss will have the greatest effect on transfer of skills. For example, a study led by Huczynski and Lewis supported these findings, concluding that people who feel a high degree of support from their supervisors report a higher level of motivation to attend and learn from training opportunities.[2] These studies underscore the importance of *you* in the development process. If you are engaged, active, and involved in leadership development, those around you will develop and grow in their abilities.

Unfortunately, many organizations spend far too little time preparing their key people for the significant roles they play. These managers have been our frequent clients and report any number of challenges to us: "We need more support"; "I don't know how to coach"; "Change is overwhelming me"; "I don't have the power to reward good performance"; "I do not have the time"; "I am not a babysitter"; "The nuts and bolts of managing performance are beyond me." *The Little Book of Leadership Development* is designed to help you address these and similar concerns and accelerate leader potential in your team members.

LEADERSHIP DEVELOPMENT IN A NUTSHELL

Like the term *leadership*, leadership development has no consensus definition. However, we suggest that leadership development is a continuous process to expand the learning and performance capacity of people in organizations and communities to meet shared goals and objectives. To develop even mediocre skills at anything takes deliberate coaching, practice, and reflection. Could an Olympic gymnast be developed when provided with feedback only twice a year? Could a world-class chef? Of course not. Developing leadership capacity is the same as changing any other behavior or activity—it takes consistent coaching, practice, and reflection. Yet many organizations, divisions, agencies, communities, and departments are not structured to facilitate these steps. As a result, people spend years in organizations and communities with few opportunities to truly develop and grow as the Olympic gymnast or culinary master does.

LEADERSHIP DEVELOPMENT EVERY DAY—OUR MODEL

As you think about a leadership development system, we would like to place the image of a flower in your mind. If you are like us, perhaps some flowers have died under your watch. Amazing, given the fact that, in essence, they simply need sunlight and water. It's so simple. Your development system is no different. It will need water and sunlight to grow. It will need your time and attention—not a lot—but enough for it to grow.

The system we present is one way to develop the leadership capacity of the individuals with whom you work each and every day. The "classroom" is the work environment, and the facilitator is you, the manager. Changing how you approach your role will not only develop the leadership capacity of those around you, but it will likely increase their productivity as well. This may actually *decrease* your workload in some areas so that you can spend the time on activities where your unique expertise is called for. Though easing your own workload should not necessarily be your ultimate goal, it does imply that you've successfully delegated important work to others and is reflected in improved organizational performance. In other words, leaders create *more* leaders.

We propose six steps to implement your system of leadership development.

> ## BOX 1. OUR SIX-STEP MODEL
>
> **1.** Get your own shop in order.
>
> **2.** Build your leadership development system.
>
> **3.** Involve others.
>
> **4.** Manage the system.
>
> **5.** Evaluate the system.
>
> **6.** Add new pieces with caution.

Step 1:
Get your own shop in order.

Step one is to get your own shop in order. As you read this book, reflect on your own strengths and weaknesses as a leader. If you are not aware of these and not willing to work on them, very few of the suggestions contained in this (or any other) book will be of benefit. Why? For one primary reason: Our entire model is created on a foundation of trust. Those around you must trust that you have their best interests at heart. This is important because, as you design your system of leadership development, team members must honestly have confidence in you as their guide.

Did you ever have a coach you did not trust? How did you feel? How did you respond? How effective were you? Likely, your motivation and enthusiasm were diminished. Do you have any of those dissatisfied team members around you? What part do *you* play in their dissatisfaction? If it is for reasons out of your control, that may be reality, but, before moving forward, look within. Work to imagine why they could perceive you to be a part of their problem. After all, perception is reality. Talk with friends, your own manager, and former co-workers and see what they have to say. If those with whom you work know that you care and that you want to improve, they will be more likely to buy in to the process and improve themselves.

Note that this is hard work. Not only is it difficult to hear what others think of you, but it can be difficult to change your behavior. One leader with whom we worked was "picking up the pieces" after receiving feedback from those with whom she works. She acknowledged the initial surprise of hearing some feedback that challenged her self-image as a leader. In response, she worked with others to change those areas she hoped to improve. This was a win-win opportunity; she improved her abilities, and those around her benefited from the changes. And there were some "secondary gains" here—her honesty and desire to change rubbed off on others. This is a great example of leadership in action.

Step 2:
Build your leadership development system.

The second step in the process is to build your leadership development system. This will take on a different form for each of our readers. As you read the 50 tips in this book, flag the ideas and concepts that you currently practice or could practice, as well as the ones that are not realistic at this time. We would be fooling ourselves to think that all organizations are alike and that one size fits all.

Some of you are in large organizations, some small, some with a supportive environment for development, and others not. There are simply too many variables. However, together we will create a leadership development system tailored to your department and your organization. We recommend beginning with one or two changes at first.

Psychologically, when any of us overestimates the number or intensity of changes we can realistically make, there is a higher probability of failure than if we selected something more manageable. Consider one study by researchers that found that individuals make the same New Year's resolutions over and over, and vow to discontinue their vices each year for ten years running on average.[3] And 60 percent give up after the first week. Why? Because the goals they set for themselves were unrealistic, like trying to lose weight, quit smoking, and train for a marathon at the same time.

Both of us have been in the management trenches and understand the significant obstacles to change that can push us in directions away from the targeted course. That's the reason for moving slowly and ensuring wins. Remember, this is a long-term endeavor. We suggest the **LD50 Snapshot** found at the back of this book to help you identify which of the 50 tips you plan to prioritize.

Step 3:
Involve others.

Third, you need to involve others. Ask people on your team what they think about their own development needs and see if your perceptions are in alignment with theirs. This is an important discussion to have because others will be part of the process. Furthermore, it is wise to remember the adage "People support what they help create."

One leader recently asked why his strategic planning process was failing. He wondered if the organization should change its vision, maybe tweak the mission, and perhaps develop more concrete goals. In an "aha" moment, he discovered that only executives were participating in the effort. Yes, there was communication to inform others of decisions, but nothing that really involved people in meaningful ways. In response to this insightful moment, he engaged people by involving them in significant decisions that affected their work lives and involved representatives from various constituencies in meaningful ways as part of the process. This increased buy-in to the strategic planning process and its ultimate success.

If you hope to develop a system outside the scope of your unit, department, or community, it is important to involve key constituents. Who has the ability to assist or squelch your efforts? Think of strategic partners who have the political capital to make or break what you are trying to do. Politics is something to consider seriously. Some believe politics is evil and should not be played. We disagree. In certain circumstances, leaders actually do the opposite—they extol the virtues of politics at work. Detecting the complex web of relationships that defines the way things really get done can present a daunting challenge, but it is one that any successful manager must meet. Think of politics not as a negative dynamic, but one that will allow you to ethically drive the initiatives that are important to you and your staff.

In their book *Manager's Desktop Consultant*, Essex and Kusy identify four key questions that leaders should ask themselves to truly understand the political system in their organizations:[4]

1. What are the ways success is measured in your organization?

2. How much time is given for results to be obtained?

3. What are the decision-making processes for choosing and driving key decisions?

4. How much risk is tolerated for failed attempts at change?

Step 4:
Manage the system.

Next, be cognizant of how you will manage the system. This does not need to be overly complicated; there's no need to create or purchase a new software program. A leadership development system specifically tailored to meet the needs of your unit or department will likely work the best. In fact, this may be one of the first developmental assignments given to your team. A word of caution—until these changes are imbedded into the culture, *pay very close attention to the process.* While delegation is critical in many venues, early on in this process keep a close eye on progress and follow through with those individuals in charge of various aspects of your system. Add this as a topic for discussion at select staff meetings and ensure that team members are following through with their tasks. Host a discussion on how members of the group will hold one another accountable so, when you need to, you can refer back to the conversation later.

Managing the system is where the rubber meets the road and it will need your close attention in the beginning. If you fail to manage the system, in the end there will be little or no system to manage. It will likely fail. We have experienced this personally, not only as consultants but also as leaders in organizations. Here, we have discovered that short, purposeful check-ins are excellent ways to manage the leadership development system. In particular, it's not just about including the agenda items related to the "real" work we do in organizations but, just as important, it's about including space for people to discuss their own leadership development activities.

One group of team members recently asked themselves fundamental questions such as:

▶ How will we communicate?

▶ How will we confront each other?

▶ How will we ensure one another's development?

The team discussed such concerns as:

▶ When working with me, there are four things you should know . . .

▶ In the past year, areas I feel I have grown in are . . .

▶ My areas of weakness include . . .

These conversations ensured that everyone was developing with some intentionality. At times, the conversations were difficult but, in the end, everyone knew where each other stood and what they were working on to improve. Ultimately, the activity fostered self-awareness. Amazingly, when the group members "checked in" with one another, each individual usually mentioned aspects they needed to work on.

Step 5:
Evaluate the system.

Along with managing the system, spend some time evaluating the system periodically. Do so at least once a month in the beginning. Ask questions such as "How are we doing?" or "What is working well?" Like managing the system, evaluating the system is an essential step—always. If your team is dissatisfied or feels that a certain activity is not working, this needs to be revealed and discussed. Otherwise, the whole process becomes a joke and people will not take it seriously.

It's likely that the way we have presented the ideas in this book will not mesh exactly with your situation—so expect that some adjustments will have to be made along the way and know that there will be bumps in the road. As consultants, we would rather get these needed changes out in the open than have them fester and impede progress later. Think of this stage in the process as the "continuous improvement" component of your developmental planning. This is an often overlooked and undervalued stage of the process. On the contrary, challenge your team to ensure that it is meeting their needs and helping them grow.

Step 6:
Add new pieces with caution.

Once you have rooted one or two of the 50 tips into your culture, begin thinking about adding new pieces to the system. However, only do so if you feel you have accomplished the first five stages successfully. This will be an important discussion with your team. If you and your team determine that additional components should be introduced, reintroduce the six stages and begin the process again.

Implementing our system is a start. There may be other steps in the process; they will likely present themselves along the way.

USING THIS BOOK

Here are a few additional suggestions for using this book. Remember that the tips will not always be a perfect fit for you. It is expected that some adjustments will need to be made. However, approach each of the tips with this question in mind: *How could this tip work in my environment?* By thinking about the possibilities, you will open your mind to new ideas. In the end, you may determine that a suggestion is not appropriate; however, at least you and your team will have thought through the possibilities and potential rather than only the obvious limitations or barriers.

Don't feel the need to read the book from cover to cover—put the book down and reflect. If one tip hits you, ask others whom you trust if they think this is something relevant for your team to work on. After hearing their suggestions, write all of them down in a sort of brainstorming mode and revisit "Box 1. Our Six-Step Model." Often, people begin too soon—better to explore a number of possibilities before choosing one or two.

To remove yourself from the notion of having to read all of this book at once, read the last few tips, some in the middle, and then some at the beginning. This will help you get out of the mind-set that leadership development is a recipe.

Some of the tips seem rather simple and they are—in theory. However, we are amazed at how often they do not exist in the organizations with which we work and consult. If you find yourself saying, "That's easy. It's nothing new," great. Then ask yourself how well it is working in your department. If the concept is already in place, wonderful. If not, it may be one of the first you prioritize with your team. Many of the tips are based on leadership and management theory, but our goal is to present them in a user-friendly manner. One word of caution—do not overthink or overcomplicate these tips. They are designed to be simple and easy additions that align with the flow of your department. Resist the urge to put a lot of structure and complexity around the system. Keep it simple.

Some tips are short and to the point and others have a story or more detail associated with them. In essence, our goal is to provide you with a quick read based on sound advice. There is great power in each of these tips and some may read at times as common sense. However, as we have learned in our practice and research, *common sense does not always equal common practice.*

OUR 50 WAYS TO BRING OUT THE LEADER IN EVERY EMPLOYEE

In his book *Learning to Lead,* leadership scholar Jay Conger divides leadership development into four approaches: skill building, conceptual understanding, personal growth, and feedback.[5] *Skill-building* activities help a team member develop capacity in a specific task, such as public speaking. *Conceptual understanding,* often linked with classroom training, aligns closely with the theory of leadership or related topics. *Personal growth* opportunities are those that challenge participants to reflect on their behaviors, values, and desires. Essentially, the purpose of these activities is to increase self-awareness and emphasize self-exploration. The final approach to leadership development are activities or programs where *feedback* constitutes a large portion of the time and emphasis is placed on measuring skill in a wide range of leader behaviors. As you can imagine, there is overlap in each of these four approaches. For instance, a personal growth opportunity can lead to feedback and additional skill building, which all lead to a higher level of conceptual understanding.

We have divided our tips into these four categories and also added a fifth, which we call *modeling effective leadership*. These are tips for you as a leader. Effective leaders walk their talk and model the way. We believe that these tips, if implemented, will model leadership for those on your team. Included within each of these tips are well-studied behaviors that embody an effective leader—communication, inspiration, coaching, setting clear expectations, and so forth. We believe that by your example you will create a culture where others will develop and grow.

Development by Modeling
Effective Leadership

[1]

Clarify Team Expectations

RESEARCH INDICATES that leaders who set clearly defined expectations and agreed-on levels of performance are more likely to get positive results than leaders who don't.

This is an essential concept for you and your team. It seems so obvious, but think about it for a moment: What does your boss think of the work you are doing? Are your best interests at heart? Are expectations explicitly stated? Now, returning to your department and those who work for you, what are the perceptions of *your* team members? Are they shared perceptions? In other words, what would they think of the statements in "Box 2. Clear Expectations"? Would they respond with disagreement, neutrality, or agreement?

Could members of your team answer these questions with confidence? In our experience, for many supervisors, the answer may be no. Your team needs to know your expectations, goals, vision, and, most important, how each individual adds value. Better yet, develop these as a group. This may seem over the top, but in the end, people support what they help create. This tip will help you *gain commitment, not simply compliance*. The more your team members are part of developing group norms, the more they will buy in to them.

BOX 2. CLEAR EXPECTATIONS

I disagree, am neutral, or agree with the following statements:

1. I have a job description that clearly describes my responsibilities.

2. I receive consistent coaching from my supervisor on the work I produce.

3. I have a clear picture of what my supervisor expects of our team.

4. I have a clear picture of what my supervisor expects from me.

5. I have clearly defined goals.

[2]

Model the Way

SOCIAL LEARNING THEORISTS who study how we learn found that when children watched violent TV shows and saw people rewarded for this violence, they were more likely to demonstrate violent behavior. In a similar vein, if you are unethical, it is to be expected that those around you will see this behavior and, in some unfortunate cases, model it, as well. A great barometer for this is how you spend the organization's money when traveling. Another is what you say about others in your organization. Do you put other departments and individuals down? If so, it's likely others on your team will, too. Emotions and behaviors are contagious.

As a leader, people will use you as a model of how to function in the organization. Think about the departments with which you have the most difficulty. Is it a reflection of the leader? Does the environment they foster affect your feelings toward those departments? Are they living up to their potential? Are they modeling what your organization values? Turn your attention to departments that you respect. What are the differences among the leaders and departments?

Now, critically examine your own department. What are people's perceptions of your team? Is your department one that people rely upon? Is it respected? The environment and culture you create will often determine success or failure. Frequently, we subconsciously recruit (and retain) people who are similar to ourselves. Take a close look at yourself. Are the behaviors, policies, and cultural norms modeled by you developing others? Are they behaviors that will allow others to succeed and progress within the organization?

An excellent test of this process is to really observe how people react to you. Consider team meetings, one-on-one sessions with your team members, and even large social events. If you can't get a "pulse" on this, we suggest you ask others for their feedback. Of course, it certainly depends upon whom you ask. So, ask others who are not likely to give you what you want to hear, but will give you honest and meaningful feedback. Then, change those areas of your style that you would not want modeled by others. You don't have to do this subtly. It's perfectly okay (and we suggest this) to tell others what you are doing and why. Honesty is something you want modeled, as well.

[3]

Recognize and Reward Achievement

H OW DO YOU REWARD and recognize your team? Let's face it, reward and recognition are motivators for some individuals. It's a fundamental part of human nature to seek and respond to rewards. What is rewarded in your organization? What is rewarded in your department? We often work with organizations that talk about the importance of employee recognition, but rarely do we encounter an organization that consistently follows through. All too often, we learn that our clients only reward results, no matter what kind of collateral damage they may have done in the wake of their focus on results alone. Or even worse, some leaders simply provide team members with their annual 3 percent raise regardless of development or concrete results.

We suggest that, if you hope to create a culture of continuous development in your organization, you reward people for committing to this endeavor. If you do not, "personal development" will simply become words without action in your organization. Of course, we are saying neither that the organization needs to spend millions on reward systems, nor that you as the leader must develop an elaborate scheme for recognition and rewards.

Throw the work back to your team members. Ask them to develop a simple system that works within your budget and acknowledges those who continually grow and develop in their roles. Encourage team members to brainstorm rewards and then have them attach their names to those areas that are most significant to them. Yes, money may come out on top. If you have power over this, great.

If not, it's important to remember that money is only a short-term motivator. For true long-term motivation factors, look beyond money.

The best thing about reward and recognition is that it doesn't need to cost a penny. Get creative. One organization we worked with relied heavily upon peer recognition. Each month, an employee would pass along a simple award to another employee, and so on—classic peer-to-peer recognition. The award is not necessarily important. What is important to note is that the award was developed by team members. Staff members chose the award, and they chose the recipients month after month. What could this look like in your department? If not given monthly, could it be a quarterly award? Could the entire group vote on the recipient? The details are not important—let your team figure those out. What is important is that you have facilitated reward and recognition in your department, something we could all use more of. Something we all appreciate. Something that makes people feel good about the work they do.

[4]

Model Effective Confrontation

ANYONE IN MANAGEMENT knows that difficult conversations are a major part of the game. For a new manager (and even seasoned ones) these conversations can be difficult to navigate and, in our experience, people work more from their "default" style than an intentional approach, depending on the context. For instance, a manager who tends to avoid conflict, as a default, will likely bring this to the workplace as well. Of course, in some instances avoiding conflict may be appropriate, but in others not. In all likelihood, you have worked for someone with this default approach and, as a result, problems festered and the culture suffered.

In all reality, there are five simple approaches to conflict that include competing/forcing, accommodating, collaborating, avoiding, and compromising.[6] It is important to underscore, once again, that each of these styles has a time and a place. In addition, each one of us likely has one or two that we "go to" on a consistent basis. Likewise, there are others that you are less versed in. For instance, avoiding conflict may be difficult for an individual conditioned to always use a more combative style. The five styles are:

▶ **Competing/Forcing**—When an individual employs a competing/ forcing style, his primary objective is to get his way—oftentimes, regardless of what others think. Of course this can cause hard feelings or make others feel "walked upon," but at times this is a necessary approach to be heard, as when others are taking advantage, when others are in danger, or when immediate compliance is required.

21

▶ **Accommodating**—Individuals who employ an accommodating style want to please people and spend a lot of energy meeting the needs of others—often in an attempt to maintain a sense of harmony. The downside of this style is that the accommodator can get walked on by others.

▶ **Collaborating**—Often called the "win-win," this approach to conflict creates space for mutual dialogue. By doing so, parties examine how the needs of each can be met. The great benefit of this approach is that mutual needs are met and this approach identifies new options not previously considered.

▶ **Avoiding**—Managers who avoid conflict do not confront the necessary interpersonal challenges that exist in an organization. Ultimately, this approach allows problems to persist.

▶ **Compromising**—The objective of this approach is to make a quick decision. However, a challenge may be that each party must "give up" something, and in the end, no one is happy. Likewise, in an effort to make a quick decision, the solution may not always be the best long-term approach.

We imagine that each of these is simple enough to understand. However, mastery of each style is incredibly challenging. In real time, people often revert to their defaults versus intentionally *choosing* an approach that may be the best fit for the situation. What is your default? How does that help and hinder you as a leader? How does it stall progress for your team?

[5]

Provide Challenge _and_ Support

YOU HAVE HEARD these terms before. However, it is important to step back and think of the level of challenge and support each of those working for you has. Do some team members feel overwhelmed and undersupported? Are others supported, but not necessarily challenged? In our experience, we have found that, for each person, this invisible line is different. One size does not fit all, because each of us is unique (e.g., work ethic, stamina, level of intelligence, and personality). Some of these differences are "nature" (inherent in our personalities) while others are "nurture" (based on our life experiences and environment).

When people try to manage with a one-size-fits-all approach, they simply cannot get the best out of each individual. It is much more complicated than that. Challenging experiences help individuals develop and grow. They push people out of their comfort zones and into new places. We call this "the edge." You know you are at your edge when you have that nervous feeling in your stomach, a feeling of uncertainty as to how things will turn out. For some, this may be public speaking; for others, it may be a deadline or a sales goal. Along with challenge, a supportive working environment develops trust and lets people know that they will be safe when they are placed in situations outside their comfort zones. Few people take risks in an environment where they don't feel supported. Have you ever worked in a place like that?

Applying this concept to organizations specifically, Buckingham and Coffman demonstrated that when people get a new job they are typically most excited about the organization, but they leave because of a lousy boss.[7] Think about it. When you get a new job, most of the conversations revolve around the role and the organization. You might have mentioned a little about your boss (if you met her during the interviewing process). However, when you left the position, you likely spoke less about the organization and more about your boss.

Again, people leave organizations because of bad bosses. In their book *The High Impact Leader*, the authors suggest that the latest research indicates leaders who display and develop confidence, optimism, hope, and resiliency in others are effective in their leadership roles.[8] Do you do this for those around you? Or are you a disruptive and uncivil leader who leads with toxic behaviors, as described in Kusy and Holloway's book *Toxic Workplace! Managing Toxic Personalities and Their Systems of Power?*[9]

[6]

Keep the Troops in the Loop

YOU ATTEND ALL KINDS of organizational meetings. If you shared only 50 percent of the information you received in these meetings, your team members would likely know significantly more about the organization than they currently do. Often, managers do not communicate this information back to their teams.

Take notes and be sure that you share pertinent information about the strategic plan, goals, and organizational announcements with those around you. Nothing is more frustrating than working for a manager who does not communicate organizational or community information. This will diminish the trust your team has in your abilities. Your team looks to you to keep them in the loop. If they do not get information from you, they will likely get it from the grapevine, where the message is uncontrolled and often distorted.

Keep your team members up-to-date with the latest information, and you will be developing their knowledge, skills, and attitudes about the organization. Most important, if there is bad news, they should hear it from you. After communicating information, be sure to leave time for questions and space for team members to express frustrations, fears, and discontent. Do your best to be in that conversation so you know where they stand.

What if there is nothing to report? Many managers would do nothing. You should do the opposite. Letting the team know that you have nothing to report does two things:

► It lets the team know you haven't forgotten about them.

► It builds trust that you are walking your talk by doing what you said you would do.

So what system do you have in place to ensure that your team is in the loop and aware of organizational decisions, directions, and challenges?

[7]

Check in with a Thought of the Day

MANY MANAGERS PASS ALONG a thought of the day to those with whom they work: a virtual "stand-up" meeting if you will. This e-mail could be a quote, a message related to your business, or simply a reminder to your team. Whatever the case, a simple daily thought to your team members is a great way to develop their knowledge and skills. If you don't feel as though you have the time, then see if someone on your team is willing to complete this task.

You could also rotate the duties because, as we will discuss, teaching is the highest form of learning. Connecting with those with whom you work, even through e-mail, lets them know that you care and are accessible. On hectic days, you may even let your team know of a couple of good times to pop in with questions. Research by Kelloway and colleagues found that effective leadership could be detected through leaders' e-mails. Make your e-mails upbeat and encouraging to those around you.[10] Remember, emotions and the tone of your correspondence can make all the difference in the world.

This approach is a good way to manage virtual teams, as well, because it makes team members feel in touch. However, remember that e-mail/texting can be abused, and some are better at reading these regularly than others. Be sure the daily e-mail is brief, is to the point, and has meaningful information for the receiver. Otherwise, it may fall victim to the "automatic delete." Make this the first task you complete each morning.

[8]

Realize Your Team Is <u>Your</u> Customer

"How may I better serve you?"—all of us love to hear this question. Within those six words is a message that you are important and valued. When we don't feel valued, we may take our business (and careers) somewhere else. When we do feel valued, respected, and cared for as a consumer, we are more likely to go back. Any successful business owner knows this—after all, it is more costly to recruit new customers than it is to retain current ones.

This concept applies to leadership, as well. If you have a team of committed individuals (not simply compliant team members), in all likelihood you have a productive and enthusiastic team. In essence, you are a customer service agent for those who work for you. You are their main contact with the organization, and if you act in a customer service–oriented manner and create a culture where service to others is the expectation, chances are your team will do the same. Ask your team how you may better serve them and then follow through. This is a two-part endeavor—ask and then follow up. Pretty soon, those team members who are self-aware will be asking you this question. What a gift. This is a simple suggestion that can pay huge dividends for you and your team members.

We suggest that you ask this question in different ways. One leader has used these questions in the name of service delivery and leadership development:

► Am I providing what you need right now?

► Am I being an obstacle or a help with this project?

► How can you best use me here?

Remember, asking the question is not enough. Whenever possible, you must follow through on the suggestions—otherwise, you lose credibility and trust. If you cannot follow through on the request, be sure to say why.

[9]

Use the Pygmalion Effect

HERE'S A PRETTY COOL CONCEPT known as the Pygmalion Effect. If you haven't heard of it specifically, you probably have witnessed it in action. Leadership scholar Bernard Bass suggested that

> In its most general form, the Pygmalion Effect is a performance-stimulating effect. People who are led to expect that they will do well will be better than those who expect to do poorly or do not have any expectations about how well or poorly they will do. People tend to try to confirm rather than disconfirm positive beliefs that others have about them.[11]

If this is the case, then you should be thinking about how you communicate verbally and nonverbally with your team. A number of studies have confirmed this phenomenon. If nothing else, it is good to be aware of this theory, and how it can be used to influence others.

The application is fairly simple. Try this approach with your organizational "stars" at first. "Sculpt" their performance by recognizing their past performance and your confidence that they will continue down the same path. Another approach at the team level is to simply tell team members that you have every confidence they will shine in a challenging project. Of course, let them also know you are available as a resource as the project progresses. Leaders tend to spend far too much time with their poor performers and not enough time with their stars. The authors of *First Break All the Rules* suggest switching the time commitment between the two groups.[12] We suggest a slight alteration—spend more time with your organizational stars and remain aware of the Pygmalion Effect when working with them.

It's not solely upon organizational stars that you should focus this strategy. This can work with other levels of performance as well. We mention it in connection with the stars because in all reality there lies the greatest likelihood for success. They are usually the most motivated and at times the most neglected from a developmental perspective. We suggest spending more quality time with them, but we also suggest trying this strategy with those of other performance levels.

[10]

Coach for Performance

W E BRIEFLY MENTIONED this concept, but developing leadership is like developing a skilled athlete. Quite simply, most people need to practice to become world-class. They also need coaching. Clear expectations and goals are only the first step. Next, your team needs a supervisor who "coaches" performance on a consistent basis. If you are hoping to develop leadership capacity in those around you, sporadic and haphazard coaching is quite an absurd approach when one looks at this prospect logically. What if aspiring gymnasts received the same amount of token coaching? What would their skill levels be? Certainly not Olympic caliber. Some supervisors may say that they don't have time. We would argue that managers *need to make time*. After all, how much time could be saved if your team members were "Olympians"? What if your organization had team members with one-third more skill and leadership ability? We know managers can create better leaders within their departments. We've seen it happen.

However, there must be some intentionality behind the development. You can increase your team's level of output just as coaches can increase the output of their teams. Of course, all managers have some people with natural ability along with others who need to work at developing their skills.

There are many coaching models. We suggest keeping it simple:

▶ Set clear expectations and stretch goals.

▶ Challenge and support.

► Monitor performance.

► Provide coaching/feedback in small, concrete chunks.

► Follow up consistently and repeat the process.

[11]

Facilitate a Culture of Accountability

How MANY TIMES throughout your career have you watched those around you not being held accountable for what they said they would do? What is the accountability system within your department? Is there one? Would everyone working for you identify this system and, if we asked them today, would they all answer in the same manner?

Accountability is a challenging issue. It's not fun and it's often uncomfortable because it often involves confrontation. However, when team members exist in a culture that has little or no accountability, we suggest that it hurts the team in the long run. The same concept applies to parenting. How? Well, it creates bad habits, for one. You may have friends who struggle to hold their children accountable but they are sporadic and inconsistent. They ask their children to do something and struggle to follow through with the consequence when it is not done. The short-term pain of following through is too overwhelming. Children quickly learn that they do not have to follow through, and by the time they are teenagers, the parents have a mess on their hands. Accountability in the office environment is a similar concept. If no accountability system exists, then how will behaviors change? A sporadic performance evaluation? Will this truly change behavior? No.

Ask your team members how they want to be held accountable. Ask them how they can hold each other accountable. Ask them how they can hold *you* accountable. An environment in which people follow through and know that they will be held accountable is more productive and filled with individuals who clearly understand the expectations of their team and their supervisor. Adult learning theory tells us that individuals in an environment that models a desired behavior will influence those around them to behave in a similar manner. Accountability is one of those areas in which this modeling concept applies beautifully.

One of our clients reported to us the positive response she received when she asked her team members how they could hold her account-able. Not only were team members supportive of this, she received many outstanding ideas. She took detailed notes and made it a point of practicing this new approach on a regular basis.

[12]

Tap into Their Passion, Unleash the Energy

SOME PEOPLE THINK that you should keep your distance from those who work for you. Somewhere along the line, you may have been told, "Don't get too close" or "Some level of fear is good." According to the research, this is not true. You don't have to be best friends with your team members. You do, however, need to spend time getting to know them. You need to know about their goals—personal, as appropriate, and professional alike. You need to know what motivates them and how they would like to be held accountable. We say all of this because they need to know that you have their best interests at heart. Leadership scholars Bernard Bass and Bruce Avolio suggest that if your team members know that you care about them they will work harder and produce more.[13] As you look at your career, can you think of a supervisor whom you respected? We would imagine that the majority of you felt that this person had your best interests at heart. They cared about your development and challenged you. They understood when you had personal issues arise. They were flexible, yet structured, in their expectations.

If you were to line up all the people who work for you and work to understand their goals, motivations, values, and beliefs, it is likely that you would elicit responses at each end of the spectrum. For example, some come to work because of the paycheck. Others find an inherent sense of mission in the work they do. You have the challenge of leading individuals with myriad personality differences, and your ability to do it well will determine your success or failure as a leader. More important, the manager creates the culture (on a micro level) that (in part) determines how people feel when they come to work every day. All too often, organizations and leaders assume that a one-size-fits-all approach will produce a committed and competent workforce. In reality, it can take an organization only so far. Have you worked for a leader who assumed the same techniques and behaviors would motivate everyone on the same level? One-size-fits-all can take the manager or an organization only to a certain point. At some point, effective leaders dig deeper and truly get to know those around them—they learn about, and focus on, group and individual aspirations. By doing so, managers can "switch up" their approaches to meet the needs of those around them. In a strange way, this concept is akin to excellent customer service (see Tip #8: Realize Your Team Is *Your* Customer). When people treat you well, you treat them well in return, establishing a sense of mutual commitment and respect. Moving away from the one-size-fits-all style of leadership will move those with whom you work from mere compliance to commitment.

Remember, you're developing leadership potential in others, so you want to do two things. First, identify the knowledge, skills, or abilities you wish to see more of. Second, find the right motivator to help your team members grow in this area. Next, employ Tip #10: Coach for Performance.

[13]

Hold Standing One-on-Ones

THIS MAY SEEM like a very obvious tip. It is. However, in our experience, there are managers who are not meeting with their individual team members on a regular basis. Don't believe us? Simply ask five friends outside your organization whether or not they have regularly scheduled one-on-one meetings with their staff. And if they don't, why not? We are confident you can think of the reasons: lack of time or resources, differing locations, too many tasks on the to-do list, and any number of other excuses. Yes, we truly regard these as excuses. We had previously mentioned that managers should be great coaches (Tip #10: Coach for Performance). After all, they're charged with aligning and mentoring staff to help meet the organization's strategic objectives and be good organizational citizens. Right? Often, this is not the case. Think about it for a moment. How often do you meet with your supervisor? Is your supervisor guiding your development and growth in the organization? We hope so.

As the book *The Leader's Voice* asserts, "the biggest problem with leadership communication is the illusion that it has occurred."[14] Think about this statement for a moment. If we were to ask a former supervisor of yours if she or he had been open and available, we imagine receiving a response like, "Yes, I always told that person to feel free to set a meeting." However, your perception and experience might have been much different—and you may have eventually given up. Your supervisor may have said the right things but had a more difficult time linking actions with words.

Standing one-on-ones can be part of the solution. Maybe not every week, but managers we know who really want to develop their team make this a priority. If time is an issue, schedule the meeting. As with any good meeting, the discussion should end when the objectives of the meeting have been accomplished. Finally, remember to include some time during this meeting for developmental conversation. You can certainly incorporate many of the tips we suggest in this book during the one-on-one meeting.

[14]

Help Make Their Vision a Reality

W E ALL HAVE dreams and aspirations. It's safe to assume that many of us have yet to realize them. However, the more you know about the dreams and aspirations of those with whom you work, the better you will assist your team members along their respective journeys.

There are several leaders with whom we have worked as consultants who have taken this strategy and really run with it. One leader asked her team members to write a short memo regarding where they would like to be in their careers. She asked them to do this from two contexts—from within the organization and from within *any* organization. One may wonder specifically about the second context. The reason for this is that individuals are often hindered when one considers only the current organization. By truly exploring outside the organizational boundaries, true visioning can occur.

In the situation mentioned above, she (and her team) discovered many components important to career success. In general, they found that some of their assumptions about where they were or would like to be were erroneous. Second, they discovered that they could get there faster by first addressing this vision in incremental steps. Third, team members found support from others as they shared their visions, found common components to them, and offered each other as resources in selected circumstances.

We hope this story helps emphasize the notion that visions are not illusory. By considering both in-organization and outside-organization contexts, sharing these with others, and breaking them down into manageable steps, visions can be realized more quickly.

Finally, aligning your team members' vision with the needs of the organization can provide a concrete base for one's own vision. Helping team members see that their efforts now can link to their long-term goals and objectives has great power.

[15]

Solidify Their Learning

A S DISCUSSED in the introduction, the supervisor is crucial when it comes to behavior change and transfer of training back on the job. This only makes sense. You are their coach. Following a learning experience, ask your team members what they learned, what they would like to change, and how you can assist them in the process. By doing so, they will trust that you support their efforts and care about their development.

Support needs to be behavioral. For example, if you are sending people to training, don't let it begin and end there. Before the training, ask them what they hope to gain from the experience and how it applies to their role. When they return, ask them to quickly report on this. Take one of their goals and make it part of their performance review process. And finally, support them by giving them a stage to report their learning to others on the team. There may be hesitancy with some individuals to report to others what they have learned—maybe even some level of anxiety. This is good, because challenges of this sort can turn into real growth experiences.

It's important to remember that leaders must think of the growth potential not only of the active participant in a conference (the person attending) but also the passive recipients (individuals who did not attend but could still benefit from this learning). A small start-up company made it a policy that all learning will be shared with others. What if the training was a dud (which certainly happens)? The individuals attending were expected to share why the learning bombed, what their expectations were, and how they might achieve the learning in other ways (e.g., online resources, books, journal articles, and so forth). We hope you see that the leader in this specific example is being concrete in the types of behavioral support needed to enhance learning.

Development Through Skill Building

[16]

Stretch Your Team—Always

How often have you said, "It's just easier to do things myself?" In reality, most of us have spent the extra hours doing a task ourselves, believing it would get done more quickly and efficiently that way. However, if you look around, there are probably people willing to take on more work. These are team members who want to take their experiences and skills to the next level. Slowly opening the door for them to help you accomplish everything on your plate is a great way to develop those around you. If you do not have the time, explain projects in small steps or schedule a time to explain the project thoroughly.

In other words, develop those around you by offering "stretch assignments." At any given time, *all* team members should be working on at least one project that is taking their skills to the next level—a project just outside their comfort zone. Take some time, develop a plan, and, little by little, your time will free up and those around you will develop. Remember, you need to be specific about the objectives and implement the simple Coach for Performance model we suggest in Tip #10.

You also need to make sure you are available for questions. This takes a little time in the beginning but, in the end, you will actually have *more* time. Stretch assignments are perhaps the most widely used development tool, according to some leadership experts. Researchers McCall, Lombardo, and Morrison studied executives to determine critical developmental experiences in their careers.[15] The vast majority felt that experience was the greatest educator. Other studies have found similar results. Many executives attributed learning from assignments such as project task forces, line-to-staff switches, starting a venture from scratch, turn-it-around jobs, and a leap in scope.

For assignments to have "stretch," two variables should be present. First, they should be challenging, not just work for work's sake. Second, stretch assignments should provide team members with opportunities to try out new skills, behaviors, and thinking.

Several of our clients include this topic in their standing one-on-one's (see Tip #13) with direct reports, specifically regarding the progress they are making toward accomplishing their stretch assignments. Once this approach is consistently applied, as these leaders have done, it quickly becomes part of your team's culture.

[17]

Switch It Up

I F YOU TAKE a close look at your team, you will likely notice that many of the tasks being accomplished are often completed by the same people. A variation of the stretch assignment (see Tip #16: Stretch Your Team—Always.) is to facilitate an environment where, every once in a while, team members swap tasks and learn about what the others have been working on. This approach will not only increase the skill levels of those in your department but also help them better understand the organization. Better yet, team members will understand the constraints and complexities that others have to work through on a daily basis. In addition, a different set of eyes may help develop breakthroughs and remove barriers based on one's own organizational relationships.

A variation of this idea occurred when one of our clients from a high-tech manufacturing company used a "different set of eyes" to troubleshoot and brainstorm. She had her team brainstorm how others in different disciplines or areas of the company might address a particular issue. For example, one of the issues they were trying to solve was how to improve service to their internal customers. She asked the group, "How would a marketing person solve this problem? How would a human resource specialist address it?" This process was quite successful in helping others problem solve in new and creative ways.

Try experimenting with this approach on smaller projects at first. After some time, talk with team members and listen to what they have gained from the experience. If it fits your culture, attempt this with larger projects, as well.

[18]

Have Them Lead the Team

WEEKLY/MONTHLY MEETINGS are a great opportunity for your team members to gain experience leading your team. Let each member of the team fill this role for a month or some other period of time. Allow them to be responsible for developing the agenda, leading the meeting, and disseminating the minutes. After a full rotation among the staff, your team will better understand how difficult it is to set an agenda and guide a group of people with many opinions and competing commitments. More important, they will better understand how to lead a meeting and will actually become more effective team members.

As their leader, this exercise provides you the opportunity to sit back, watch the dynamics, and be a participant in the process. You will have an opportunity to coach your team members individually (and the team as a whole). A team that better understands these skills will not only be more effective in the larger organization, they will be more in tune with each other. This tip will take some time but, after a few months, you will have new perceptions of people at your meetings—they will be more aware of the issues and run better meetings.

With some coaching and feedback, team members' skills will improve before your eyes. It is no different from coaching Little League or an Olympic swimmer. Team members need to know the skills and must have feedback on their progress.

If this is a new technique for you, it may be helpful to review some of the ground rules of running an effective meeting:

GROUND RULES OF RUNNING AN EFFECTIVE MEETING

▶ Distribute the agenda ahead of time. We often hear from our clients about this one. Our estimation is that 50 percent of leaders do not do so. What is most amazing is that it takes so little time. Many of our clients have templates for this, along with a "pop-up" on the computer to remind them to distribute the agenda. One leader told us that he not only rotates meeting facilitators but also the responsibility for the agenda and note taking.

▶ State how much time is being allotted to each agenda item and whether it is an actionable item or merely a topic for discussion.

▶ If it looks like an agenda item will go beyond the allocated time, stop and ask the team members how they would like to proceed. If they say that they wish to continue discussing the item, ask them which items to eliminate from that day's agenda. If they want to table the discussion, ask how and when they would like to resume it. If they wish to complete the item within the time allocated, ask them how this will be accomplished (e.g., leader makes decision, voting, consensus, or the expert in the group makes the decision).

▶ Be sure that team members leave the meeting with clear action items and due dates, and *have the note taker place these items on the next agenda for follow-up.*

▶ Finally, *quickly* meet with the facilitators periodically and coach them on what they did well and which areas need to be improved. You might even consider using one or more of the coaching models (see Tip #26: Foster Critical Reflection and Tip #46: Create a Culture of Feedback), which can be integrated here. Another technique is to ask the facilitators what they believe went well and what could be improved.

[19]

Create Great Communicators

L EADERS MUST communicate their thoughts, ideas, and dreams—often with little warning. In an effort to help your team members develop these skills, it is imperative that they have time presenting in front of the group. This is no small feat, because some research shows that people's fear of public speaking is greater than that of dying. In fact, Jerry Seinfeld joked in one of his comedy routines that most people at a funeral would rather be in the casket than give the eulogy!

Despite this common fear, public speaking is a necessary skill for leaders. After a few times through this exercise, your team will likely feel more and more comfortable. A five-minute presentation is a great way to challenge those on your team to develop a skill set needed in the world of leadership. You may get some grief on the front end of this one, but if you explain that their best interests are at heart and model the presentation first, team members will likely thank you in the end. Be sure to provide a safe environment with solid ground rules and opportunities for feedback.

One idea is to ask someone from your communications department (if your organization has one) to help guide you through the process and provide some front-end education for your team. If your organization doesn't have a communications department or if you are working in a community, we suggest that you ask someone with superb facilitation skills to help. For instance, some companies offer monthly "presentation skills" courses for those interested in developing their abilities in a safe and comfortable environment. Just remember, presentation skills can be learned and, like anything else, individuals will improve with practice and will be better prepared for a real impromptu speech.

The following tips may prove to be a simple and straightforward model for your team to use as a template for effective presentations.

BOX 3. SIMPLE PRESENTATION MODEL

Tell

Show

Do

Feedback

Do

In the "tell" phase, it's important for leaders to share with others what they hope to accomplish with the presentation. So, make sure you don't miss the opportunity to tell people what you're going to cover in a brief and concrete way. One tip for doing this is to use a number in the presentation (e.g., "Here are the three considerations . . ." or "The five best strategies for . . ." or "The four most important suggestions for improving . . ."). Interestingly, we have discovered that when we use this strategy, participants have instinctively picked up their pens and jotted down these points.

Next, "show" them what you mean. Yes, it can certainly be a PowerPoint slide, albeit one that is simple and easy to read. But don't put too many words on the slide. Use bullet points or numbers to emphasize your point. It can also be written on a flipchart page, or simply a model drawn on the dry-erase board. One of our clients tested this. She made a presentation with elaborate PowerPoint slides for a group one week, then presented to the same group the following week with only a couple of brief points on each slide. And which was the most memorable? You got it . . . the simpler one. So, save yourself some time: Use PowerPoint slides that are simple and concrete—those that truly emphasize your point—and not slides that confuse and bore participants.

Third, "do" what you are presenting. For example, if you are trying to change an engineering process, tell a story that demonstrates what you want others to do. If you are attempting to show the importance of culture in an organization, share an anecdote demonstrating clearly what you mean.

Fourth, provide "feedback" on the results you have obtained by engaging in this new strategy. Better yet, ask if there are team members who could share their learning, and then respond to it. Your comments should be constructive in nature so that there is an opportunity to pass along some wisdom.

Finally, share your own learning as to how you course-corrected—the "do" once again, if you will, after you have received feedback. You might also ask for examples of how others course-corrected when they received feedback.

[20]

Grow Their Roles

JOB ENRICHMENT provides team members with additional duties and an increased level of work content and responsibility. For example, a team member's task that was previously observed closely by you may now be carried out with more autonomy. In effect, the work itself becomes a source of motivation for the individual. Advantages noted by some are an increase in job satisfaction, decrease in costs, increase in the quality of work, increase in the quantity of output, and decrease in monotony. A natural challenge to job enrichment is that not all employees react the same or want the same out of their careers. Nonetheless, this is a simple way to develop those around you and tap into their passion (see Tip #12: Tap into Their Passion, Unleash the Energy and Tip #14: Help Make *Their* Vision a Reality).

This is a process of discovery that requires you to spend time with team members to discern their leadership goals, the expectations they have of the organization, and any obstacles they've been experiencing. The process becomes a matching game between the perceptions of the employee and the needs of the organization. One caution: Think beyond your organization's current needs. Consider what activities they may need to help them now and in the future. And one additional tip: If your organization has a strategic plan, use this as a connection point. Don't rely on the executives having the wherewithal to engage this plan. It's up to you to connect it to your employees. And leadership development is a great way to do so.

If you have team members who need to improve their project management skills, perhaps they should lead a medium-level project. If you have team members who are afraid of public speaking, it might be good to get them out there doing just that. All of these are opportunities for growth and development. The key point is that these opportunities become an integral part of their jobs. It is rare that team members fall flat on their faces. With you by their side, you will support them in ways that they perhaps could not have imagined. You are the "guide on the side" instead of the "sage on the stage." With this guiding process, your team members will be more in tune with their areas of development if taken out of their comfort zones.

A variation of this tip is to ask team members to take on small aspects of your job. What are the day-to-day tasks that eat up your time and that would serve as a developmental opportunity for someone on your team? Taking five to ten minutes to explain aspects of your job can save you hours in the long run.

[21]

Let Them Answer the "How"

YOU ARE probably faced with implementing decisions from above. We've all been there. It is called "middle management" for a reason. Often, we find ourselves in the middle, and while we may not agree with the course of action ourselves, we are charged with making it happen. If at all possible, let those implementing the policy/procedure (often those on your team) make it their own, even on the smallest level. Maybe your team sets up the timeline, looks at the project plan, and determines implementation strategies. As much as possible, get your team bought into the process. We all like to have *some* choice in how we will behave or conduct our work. Edicts from you and those above will only make the project less enticing for you and for those on your team charged with implementation.

Whenever possible, look at your team and say, "Here is the end product and these are the objectives that must be met. I am here to support you. Let me know how I can help you meet these goals." Some of you may have just twitched because you can't imagine those around you having the ability (or time) to take on the initiatives directly. Helping those around you attain a sense of ownership will foster higher levels of commitment rather than simple compliance.

One supervisor did just this. He did not get caught up in the details—he simply set clear objectives, helped those around him understand why the change was needed, and let his team design effective courses of action. Of course, he had final approval and may have included his thoughts along the way, but the team worked to decide their ultimate fate. As a result there was a greater sense of buy-in and knowledge on the team. Moreover, team members respected the fact that the supervisor trusted them to "do it their way."

[22]

Establish Action Learning Projects

IN THE BOOK *Linkage Inc.'s Best Practices in Leadership Development Handbook*,[16] the authors conclude that action learning is one of the most popular ways to foster leadership development. Essentially, action learning is a process of approaching an organizational problem with a learning perspective. With action learning there is critical and scheduled reflection of the learning associated with the project. Participants solve real organizational problems and develop and grow in the process. There is no classroomlike venue.

Action learning can accelerate learning, develop cross-functional relationships, and, most important, demonstrate a return on investment. Organizational problems or issues that could constitute action learning projects may include workforce turnover, improving processes or systems, increasing sales, resolving problems between departments, reorganization of a department or unit, increasing productivity, or visioning new areas of focus.

One important point to note is that you will need to be a champion of this process. In addition, be sure to allow time for reflection while the team is working on the project and upon completion. After all, it is through review and reflection that much of the learning occurs.

At a health-care organization in the midst of implementing new policies and procedures, organizational executives chose to use the action learning approach and the results were positive. The executives identified a number of individuals at various levels in the organization to serve on selected committees tasked with solving organizational issues. Of course there was a focus on learning as they went along.

Each executive sat on one of the committees and helped them "fast-track" decisions and solutions. This approach not only fostered an increased level of support throughout the organization, it was a new and different approach—less "top-down" than decisions made in the past. In addition, it built relationships between executives and employees who may not have worked together otherwise.

[23]

Design a Department Retreat

DESIGNING A MEANINGFUL RETREAT may seem fairly straightforward at first blush, but in actuality, the process is quite complex for a number of reasons. First, designing a curriculum that is aligned with the strategic goals of the department requires a higher level of knowledge about its inner workings. To design a process of goal setting, goal tracking, and accountability, the facilitator must have a solid mastery of curriculum development and design, facilitation, project management, goal setting, and presentation skills. Likewise, a system for continuous and ongoing monitoring of the goals developed is essential.

Another challenge is that, oftentimes, people do not look forward to attending these types of events. Why? Well, we are quite confident you have been captive to an event that you knew would a) not lead to anything long term, and/or b) was not an enjoyable use of your time. So designing a retreat that is both productive *and* enjoyable is no small challenge.

Another aspect of this tip is the actual facilitation of the event. As the person responsible for the content and delivery, influencing the team to be involved and engaged is an essential skill for an emerging leader. Facilitation differs from presentation in that the objective is not necessarily to share what *you* know but the art of capturing and mining what those *around you* know or want.

Of course, you will need to provide continuous and ongoing support to ensure a successful event, and as team members learn and grow, they will get better and better at curriculum development and design, facilitation, and follow-through.

[24]

Implement an Operating Calendar

D O YOU often feel as though you and your team are only react-
ing—always rushing to accomplish tasks and meet deadlines?
What usually happens within your department every February? How
about May? Often, managers have these answers in their head, but
those around them have no concept of what work is conducted
throughout the year—until they have been there for years.

An operating calendar is a simple tool to help you and your team
track annual projects. Simply create a document and list all major activities that occur each month. Assign someone to keep and update this
document on a regular basis. After all, the calendar will be a continual
work in progress. However, the benefits of this tip are numerous:

- ▶ The document keeps everyone on track.

- ▶ It helps people develop an appreciation for all the tasks and projects completed by your department.

- ▶ Everyone has a strong working knowledge of what must happen
  (and when) throughout the year.

- ▶ The document can serve as an accountability tool because projects
  are not checked off until they are completed (e.g., the document
  holds team members accountable and the entire team knows
  where each individual stands).

When we monitor or assess something, there will likely be a
change in behavior, even if our only intention is to monitor. Think

about it this way: You or someone you know are likely to have been on a weight-loss program at some point. Just by monitoring the intake of calories, you have a greater chance of losing weight than if you had not done so. So, all things being equal, if you monitor calories and exercise, the probability of losing weight is greater than if you just exercise. The same applies in your department.

This tip may not suit your department neatly, but how could the overall concept work for you? How could you tailor the suggestion to meet your needs? Bring your team together to discuss and then follow up with an approach the entire group suggests as a monitoring device. We have noticed that a lack of accountability within departments and organizations leads to waste and missed opportunities.

[25]

Create a Culture of Benchmarking

W HAT ARE the other organizations or communities in your area of expertise doing well? Benchmarking is a wonderful developmental activity for a number of reasons. For instance, the activity allows individuals an opportunity to get away and examine another organization. The process of benchmarking confirms what you are doing well and shines a light on what needs to be improved. Your team needs to experience and internalize what other organizations are doing. After all, with your guidance, they will likely implement what they have learned. Leaders should schedule opportunities for their teams to benchmark other companies, divisions, agencies, and departments at least twice a year. As an aside, it may be helpful to benchmark organizations outside your domain. Doing so will allow your team the chance to view other models and practices that may not exist in your industry. Several clients of ours have actually found greater success benchmarking industries different from their own. Why? For two reasons. First, without the threat of competition, people are more likely to be honest regarding their business practices. Second, it is more likely that organizations with environments different from yours are doing unique things that may be foreign to your industry. We know that necessity is the mother of invention, so this approach is a particularly good one to develop this innovative spirit.

Bottom line, benchmarking is a great way to stay ahead of the curve, whether you benchmark parallel or nonparallel industries. If your team members know what is happening in peer institutions or communities, they will be better educated and better prepared to take your organization to the next level.

Development Through
Conceptual Understanding

[26]

Foster Critical Reflection

A DULT LEARNING EXPERTS Jack Mezirow[17] and Stephen Brookfield[18] suggest that one of the primary ways adults learn is through reflection. To transform our thinking, there is a need for critical reflection. This assists learners in confronting their political, economic, social, and cultural viewpoints—becoming more aware of how these (and others) affect their views of the world.

Encouraging your team members to understand the reasoning behind policies, procedures, and cultural norms will assist them in helping the organization grow. Further, they will be in a better position to troubleshoot problems or areas of concern. Reflecting on events can help team members analyze what went well and what went wrong. All it takes is three quick questions on your part to stimulate reflection. We suggest using our "LCS" method. This is an acronym for the items in Box 4.

BOX 4. THE LCS METHOD

► What did you Learn about yourself?

► Based on this learning, what will you Change?

► Share with others how they can help in the future

In our hectic lives, many team members fly through the day without taking time to reflect, causing them to make the same mistakes and

67

engage in the same behaviors over and over. We have all seen it, but re-flection can jump-start an increased level of self-awareness. All of us have worked with people who have low levels of awareness—they have no idea that many dislike being around them. They don't even realize when they are bringing the team down. Reflection is a competency that all of us can work on continually.

What we often suggest to clients is that they take just five minutes out of a staff meeting for individuals to share their learning with others on the team. And it's not just about those projects that succeeded. This strategy can (and should) be used for those projects that did not pan out as expected. The individual will likely learn from this reflection, and so will others on the team. It is also an empowering strategy whereby "failures" are rewarded, metaphorically speaking. If you want people to reflect and share learning, it is not enough to share successes.

Leaders may also stimulate reflection on failed assignments, or at least those that were not as successful as anticipated (see Tip #50: Capture the Learning from Hardships and Failure). Interestingly, this sharing of failure has been documented in many studies, articles, and books.

[27]

Host a Book/Article Club

WE KNOW, this tip does not sound all that new and energizing. However, we struggle to find leaders who do this one correctly. When done well, these discussions are a great way to promote continuous development and growth among your team members. They can take place at a breakfast meeting or perhaps a brown bag lunch; the important thing is that those around you are continually challenged to think in new and creative ways. You may find that those interested in taking part tend to be the people willing to go above and beyond their normal responsibilities. In our opinion, the articles and books should be user-friendly and a relatively "quick read"—we all have seen book clubs crumble because no one had the time to get through a lengthy book.

In our opinion, an insightful blog post or an article from *Fast Company* or *Harvard Business Review* should be enough to stimulate conversation. Complex or cumbersome articles and books simply are not realistic when you take into account your team members' busy schedules and demands away from work. The most important aspect of this tip is the discussion that follows the reading. This should be done in a location free of distractions and at a time that does not force participants to stay after or start before their regular work hours. Learning will happen through discussion, because diverse points of view challenge all of us to widen our frames of reference.

The conversation can be started by simply asking, "How does this article (or book) relate to the work of our department?" From there, the discussion will likely flow—unless you hog the conversation and use this time as your personal soapbox. Don't! Keep in mind the

90/10 rule: You should listen 90 percent of the time and speak 10 percent of the time. The first couple of meetings may be a bit awkward, but once people get used to the idea and feel more comfortable speaking, conversation will be rich and free-flowing. You may even ask participants to come prepared with discussion questions, or ask different individuals to lead the discussion each week. But remember the 90/10 rule. Your active listening will help you better understand how your team members view their work and provide you with opportunities to make real links and connections to your area.

In one instance, we witnessed how a book club started a cultural revolution in the organization. The book club not only fostered personal growth, but the activity took its leaders to new levels. As a result, the organization took a look in the mirror and realized that it needed to change. Perhaps most notable about the activity was that the executive director led the discussion with her staff. She was an active participant and, through the discussions, she became excited about future possibilities, as well. The organization embarked on a change initiative and, in the process, developed a number of values-based programs, raised millions of dollars, and started to better live its mission.

[28]

Foster a Friendly Debate

DEBATES CAN OFTEN help individuals see different sides of an issue facing you and your team. Challenging your team to debate by discussing positions at the other end of the spectrum from their natural position is an excellent vehicle for developing employees because it helps them understand multiple perspectives.

Team members who can debate all sides of an issue intellectually are apt to think more innovatively than those who view an issue in a dualistic—absolute right or wrong—manner. We have found tremendous success with this strategy. Provide an opportunity for team members to debate issues with which they knowingly do not agree. Doing so will help team members think about the problems that face your area in a new and different way.

Another twist may be that they take on the perspective of a constituent or customer with whom you have had a difficult time. After all, you and your team do not need to agree with the positions or perspectives of your clients and constituents, but you do need to understand them if you hope to stay in the game. Simply incorporating the question "What are all sides of this issue?" will push those on your team to further investigate an issue and dig deeper than superficial explanations of complex issues.

[29]

Create an Organizational FAQ

ORGANIZATIONS HAVE many nuances, policies, and procedures. Those who have not been around a long time can truly benefit from a frequently asked questions (FAQ) resource or "fact of the day" to bring them up to speed on organizational norms, facts, policies, and events. Simply send out an e-mail to current team members and ask this question: What do you wish you had known about our organization when you started? You will get any number of interesting responses to help those new to your team acclimate more quickly. Even veterans on your team will learn a few hints, tips, and organizational nuances. Start your meetings with these interesting tidbits of information.

Another great source of information is company award applications (such as for industry awards like ISO-1000 or the Malcolm Baldrige Award). Often, these highlight a number of worthwhile and interesting facts about your organization, as well as where the organization is headed in the future. The quicker those around you can discuss the organization from top to bottom, the quicker they will be in a position to help you lead the organization.

You may be thinking: *When will I find time to develop an FAQ? Our organization is huge! Allen and Kusy are insane!* Ask those around you to help with the project. Assign it to a high performer. Or, rather than give superfluous work to this individual, assign the FAQ process to an intern.

As part of this process, remember the importance of incremental steps. You don't have to do it all right away. Find those areas that will be most effective and require the least amount of resources. This simple task could serve as a great project that can have a significant effect on your department or division. The quicker team members receive the information, the quicker they can add value to your area.

[30]

Conduct a *Quick* Case Study

A QUICK CASE STUDY can be a great development opportunity. The case study could have to do with a project, ethics, leadership, or any number of "real" organizational topics. *Harvard Business Review* has a number of case studies and a quick search on the Internet will likely yield many examples that you can share with your team.

The case study can be an opportunity to challenge team members to think in new and different ways. You could even make a small competition of it and have some fun with your team. A wonderful by-product of case studies is that they allow team members the opportunity to learn from one another in a fairly safe and nonthreatening environment. After teams have discussed how they would approach the situation, engage in a discussion of how various team members used different methods with the case. Then develop a plan of action as a group. After a few hypothetical cases, introduce real organizational issues to team members in a case analysis format. This process will help them better understand the challenges inherent in your industry. In addition, it will introduce them to the complexities of your field.

After reviewing several cases and analyzing them, one leader in a high-tech manufacturing environment developed his own case. Group members gathered data from one of the organizational issues with which they were challenged and constructed a case. They shared this electronically so they could revise, as necessary. Interestingly, while developing the case, they identified some solutions they had not considered in the past. Ultimately, they determined that the reason for this "aha!" was that the case was written for everyone to see. Developing a holistic picture led them to a system-wide solution.

Get creative and make this a competition. Challenge employees or teams of employees to identify challenges ("cases") and work to develop the best solutions. Offer a prize for the winning team and have some fun with it. Which brings up an important point: Development can be *fun* with some creative thinking on your part.

[31]

Bring in Support

PEOPLE LISTEN to experts or people in positions of authority (most of the time). Use this phenomenon to your benefit and set up an environment where thought leaders reinforce your message to team members. If your team hears the message from a vice president or an expert, it begins to sink in. So, be wise about how you reinforce your messages with the team. The more often your team members hear a consistent message, the more likely they will understand that what you are saying is important and credible.

Some of you may be thinking that this is nothing new. Well, you're right—it isn't! What may be new is that people use their own expertise and don't look to others for help. And these human resources are often located within your organization. A word of caution here: Don't select the experts solely based on the fact that they support your position. If you do, employees will see through this approach. Rather, select someone based on his or her intellect, ability to relate to a group, or any number of other variables—but not whether or not they support you. In fact, we have found that some of our clients occasionally bring in an expert who has an opposing view. This kind of juxtaposition of views is helpful in getting all issues on the table. Ultimately, this has a tendency to lessen resistance to change.

While working with a nonprofit organization, we provided this feedback to an organizational leader. The leader complained that she was sick of "being the bad guy." We suggested that she utilize her resources and ask others (consultants and board members) to help reinforce the message she was trying to communicate whenever possible. This approach not only alleviated pressure on the leader, but it also created an opportunity for people in the organization to hear the thoughts and ideas of others.

[32]

*Remain Focused on the Solutions,
<u>Not</u> the Barriers*

A S THE LEADER, you cannot let members of your team get by with simply complaining about an issue that frustrates them. We have all been part of these gripe sessions. As the leader, you need people who will be solutions focused and willing to step up and solve the problems at hand. This is leadership in action. It is easy to take shots from the peanut gallery, but leaders identify solutions that work.

As soon as you and/or your team slip into this state, step back and reframe the situation. Challenge yourself and those around you to brainstorm ways around the problem. Those who work for you will have a difficult time leading others (within your department or within the organization) until they adopt a solutions-focused attitude. Create a culture where, if someone complains, they know that they will be expected to be part of the solution.

When confronted by employees with challenges or issues facing the organization, consistently respond with the following question: "What would you suggest?" This approach will force your team members to stop, think, and become a part of the solution. Of course, as with any strategy, this can certainly be overused and abused. There certainly are times when the leader must be directive, so be sure to use this method judiciously and in the right context.

What are some of these issues in your department or organization?

[33]

Conduct After-Action Reviews

A FTER IMPORTANT EVENTS, failures, or deadlines, the most successful leaders spend time reviewing what occurred as a team. By doing so, you will create an environment of continuous improvement and feedback. As previously mentioned, this approach will assist you and your team in reflecting on what occurred.

In the military, this is called an After-Action Review. According to leadership scholar Bruce Avolio, the process has several phases and begins with a discussion of the event so that a shared meaning of what happened can be developed.[19] After this step, participants engage in a discussion of why events unfolded in the manner they did, followed by the development of alternative courses of action. Leaders who have the ability to reflect upon and chart alternative courses of action (and their consequences) are thinking at a higher level. They are more aware of the context within which they are working. This is important because, all too often, leaders do not effectively "read" the context within which they work.

Individuals can be extremely successful in one context but fail miserably as leaders in another—simply because they could not adapt their styles to new contexts. Perhaps this has even happened to you along the way. In the end, leaders, parents, teachers, sales representatives, and even fund-raisers who can accurately read the context go further in their careers. Helping your team members think through these complexities will aid in their development, and yours.

In their book *Emotionally Intelligent Leadership: A Guide for College Students*, the authors provide the following example:

Think about a sports team. You have a coach (the leader), a group of players (the followers), and the context (the league rules, the other teams, the location, the season, and so forth). The coach may use a certain style one year and experience great success given the players and the context. As team members and competing teams change, however, the coach will likely need to change her motivational style, the workouts, and her approach to the game to remain successful. If the coach is unable to understand and adapt to the needs of her players (followers) and the overall environment (the context), she may find herself in trouble.[20]

So, how do you help your team develop this capacity to debrief with the goal of parlaying the results into other contexts? One executive director of a large community-based health center encourages all his project managers first to debrief with their team with a retrospective eye—what could they have done differently to improve the project's success? Then, once these are considered, the project managers are encouraged to ask their team how these perspectives can translate into other contexts. This is the important consideration in debriefs— the application to other environments.

[34]

Help Diagnose the Challenge—
Technical or Adaptive?

IN SIMPLE TERMS, great leaders challenge those around them to learn, grow, and approach new and challenging problems creatively. They understand the importance of creating an environment that challenges individuals to "think different," as Apple would say. Leadership experts Ron Heifetz and Marty Linsky discuss the concept of adaptive challenges. Heifetz and Linsky assert that

> great athletes can at once play the game and observe it as a whole as Walt Whitman described it, being both in and out of the game. Jesuits call it contemplation in action. Hindus and Buddhists call it karma yoga or mindfulness. We call this skill getting off the dance floor and going to the balcony, an image that captures the mental activity of stepping back in the midst of action and asking, what's really going on here?[21]

Adaptive challenges are problems that do not have an easily defined technical solution. In other words, a flat tire has a technical solution with a well-defined process, while teaching a group of autocratic managers engagement strategies may not be as sequential and focused. The context and the players involved certainly can change how one adapts or not. Leading an organization through adaptive challenges is difficult work. Here is the good news: At least now you can pinpoint which kind of problem you and your team members face.

Remember, adaptive challenges require deep work. They are challenges without existing or clear solutions. There is no bridge from "here" to "there." You and your team need to build it. As a result, the group will likely determine the best course of action. We think the quote "All of us are smarter than one of us" is so true. When confronted with adaptive challenges (and organizations are filled with them), utilize collective knowledge to lay down a conceptual bridge over this chasm. A team that realizes the difference between these two kinds of problems is a team that is ahead of many others.

What do leaders need to do to help their teams understand how to address these adaptive challenges? One director we have consulted with used a simple process within her existing team meetings. Once a month during the team's regularly scheduled weekly meetings, the leader gave team members an opportunity to address particular difficulties they were having. Typically, it was one or two individuals who had the floor for about ten minutes each. During these ten minutes, a discussion emerged regarding potential ways the team member could handle a particular adaptive challenge. A few weeks after the meeting, the individual sent an e-mail to the team members about their solution. Team members have reported how much they appreciated this process and what a positive difference it made when working through adaptive challenges.

This short entry cannot do the concepts justice, so we suggest you look into the work of Heifetz and Linsky. They are on the cutting edge of what leaders do, and their thinking will challenge your team to reach new levels. To learn more about their work, visit http://www.cambridge-leadership.com/.

[35]

Transfer __School__ Work Back to __Your__ Work

ENCOURAGING THOSE in your department to return to school or attend developmental certificate programs can have a major effect on the level of thinking in your area. Like everything else, it is not a panacea, but it can be one component of a comprehensive plan for developing those around you. After all, it lets others (in this case, the school) do some leadership development for you.

The mistake that many managers make is to assume that giving individuals time off and/or paying for all or part of their schooling is enough. We have found that managers with this attitude, while certainly positive, are missing an opportunity for themselves, the individual going to school, and the organization. What we suggest is that leaders take an active role in the education of others. One of the best ways to do this is to invite those in school to link some of their academic assignments to assignments at work. This is similar to the idea sharing in other tips we have discussed (see Tip #27: Host a Book/Article Club and Tip #37: Capture and Share the Learning).

Just because someone is taking a "nonrelated" course, don't assume that it's not relevant. Many courses can be linked directly or indirectly to work—not only business courses, but also psychology, sociology, anthropology, and art history, just to name of few of the many courses some perceive as not related to work. For example, an employee of one of our client managers happened to be taking an anthropology course. One of the components of anthropology is understanding culture. This individual actually designed a plan to assess the culture of the team and then involved the team in developing action strategies to follow up on the new desired culture—all from an undergraduate anthropology course.

Likewise, team members in school will be introduced to others in the community and may bring valuable suggestions and ideas to the team. When team members have the opportunity to work and learn outside the organization, many will jump at the opportunity. In fact, if you are doing it right, team members may appreciate what they have more. Let those around you know that you care about them and their development. If a degree program seems too large, what certifications, courses, or workshops will offer opportunities for growth? Each year, your team members should take advantage of opportunities to increase their skill sets through formal education, which challenges individuals to think in new ways and apply what they have learned.

What costs will your organization cover? What are the policies and procedures? How much money is in your budget for professional development? Investigate the answers to these questions and share the opportunities with those on your team.

Development Through
Personal Growth

[36]

Foster Growth Through Personal Development Plans

PERSONAL DEVELOPMENT PLANS are a systematic road map for ongoing growth. We are confident that many of our readers are familiar with these types of plans. However, if you would like to surround yourself with individuals with high levels of leadership capacity, team members must also pay attention to "soft" goals that increase their knowledge, skills, and abilities. For instance, we can all think of people who consistently meet their goals, but their personality is abrasive—they do not play well with others. Can you visualize this person? A small way to combat this is to help co-workers pinpoint leadership competencies that can be developed. One or two goals in this area not only keep team members focused on their professional objectives, but they also help them focus on their people skills and long-term development.

Be aware that goals on paper alone accomplish nothing. Continuous development requires continuous coaching. Ask your team members to discuss their plans with you every couple of weeks— nothing more than a one-minute update on their progress—what has gone well, what has not, and why. This way, their development will stay in your thoughts, *and it will stay in theirs, too.* After all, world-class athletes improve their competencies through consistent practice and coaching. Developing leadership competencies is no different.

You may want to consider combining a 360-degree feedback instrument with personal development planning. For those of you who may be unfamiliar with this process, a "360" or "multi-rater feedback" instrument allows an individual to receive feedback from peers, supervisors, direct reports, and, in some cases, key constituents, confidentially and anonymously. In other words, a 360 allows participants the opportunity to learn how others perceive them based on a set of behaviors important to the organization. In many instances, participants will rate themselves, as well—providing an opportunity to see if and how well self-perceptions are aligned with those of others.

Participants in the 360 process are asked to develop a personal plan of action following their results (see Tip #48: Provide Development Through Assessment). The plan is then reviewed and updated on a consistent basis and, as a result, action is taken on those areas identified through the feedback process. After a period of time, the participants are rated again to gauge progress.

[37]

Capture and Share the Learning

How much money does your organization spend on conferences for team members? How much learning is lost when little or no information is shared and/or implemented when they return? As we discussed earlier, some of the best learning occurs through critical reflection on events (see Tip #26: Foster Critical Reflection and Tip #33: Conduct After-Action Reviews), and there is no better way of reflecting than to share what has been learned by others. This does not need to be a thirty-minute presentation—it can simply be a one- or two-point discussion touching on the highlights.

This tip can be a great springboard for powerful discussions, but often these opportunities are overlooked. Think back to the last conference you attended. What were the topics of four of the sessions, and what were their main points? We suspect that few readers could answer this. So ask those around you to share and use the information they have gained. You could even take it a step further and set it up as a stretch assignment (see Tip #16: Stretch Your Team—Always.) so they have to actually use what they've learned. Many training and development theorists suggest that the best way to transfer training into behavior change is by practicing the new behavior regularly and frequently.

A variation of the LCS model we described earlier (see Tip #26: Foster Critical Reflection) can be used here.

We are confident that for those who attended the seminar, telling others about the experience is an excellent review for them. Teaching is the highest form of learning and it's likely that the conversation will spark further dialogue. Bottom line, what are people doing with the information they have learned?

BOX 5. ADAPTATION OF THE LCS MODEL

Learning: What did you learn about yourself or your role?

Change: Based on this learning, what will you change?

Sharing: Share with others how they can help.

[38]

Develop Emotional Intelligence

D ANIEL GOLEMAN is credited with bringing the concept of emotional intelligence to the masses.[22] He and other researchers have discovered that emotions play an ever-present role in our working lives—more than most people originally thought. Emotional intelligence (EI) and the ability to stay in tune with, and regulate, potentially detrimental behaviors are significant variables that determine success and satisfaction in all walks of life—including personal relationships.

In essence, EI is about understanding and identifying our emotions, regulating ineffective emotions, and responding to, and being aware of, emotions in others. This is an important concept because doing so helps an individual establish positive relationships with others, which, along with trust, is a foundational concept in leadership. Similar to self-awareness, EI is about connecting with others on a deeper level.

So how is EI developed? A starting place may be a relevant reading assignment and subsequent discussion. Next, ask each team member to identify one question about the article *and* your team and begin a dialogue. If you think one member of the team could benefit more than the whole, build this activity into his or her development plan (see Tip #36: Foster Growth Through Personal Development Plans).

There are many ways to take this look within, using the core concepts of emotional intelligence as a foundation. Some learning opportunities are more expensive than others and involve more time, such as 360-degree feedback processes followed with coaching by someone trained in EI. Less expensive means are simple strategies such as providing an article on emotional intelligence for everyone to read and asking participants to share one area for improvement. Or, if the individual focus is a bit too threatening for some, and we certainly understand this, one activity we have used with our own clients is to conduct the same exercise with the team. For example, team members could share one aspect of emotional intelligence that the team is particularly good at and one that needs improvement, and then develop a potential action plan for improvement.

There are many places to turn to for more information on EI. Here are a few websites we respect and admire:

- ▶ http://www.unh.edu/emotional_intelligence/

- ▶ http://www.reuvenbaron.org/

- ▶ http://www.eiconsortium.org/

[39]

Facilitate Developmental Relationships

R ESEARCH INDICATES that individuals in organizations with formal or informal mentors are more successful in their leadership careers and in maneuvering organizational obstacles and barriers with greater ease than those without relationships of this kind. Linkage Inc. (a firm that specializes in leadership development) found that exposure to senior executives can serve as a wonderful learning experience for those in an organization.[23] Bottom line: Leadership is about relationships. Relationships can open doors and opportunities that will benefit you and your team.

Whether formal or informal systems exist within your organization, plugging your team members into the organizational network can aid in their development and potentially open doors for your department. How are developmental relationships used in your department? How could such relationships benefit those with whom you work? More specifically, how do you get people excited about the significance of developmental relationships and how do you help them do something concrete about them? Here's what we have learned from our organizational clients.

One operational vice president established the most rudimentary of systems that yielded sophisticated results. Here's what she did. Instead of setting up the development system for her direct reports, she simply established the context for this and let the group members go whichever way they believed would benefit them. She gathered the group and shared some of the research about the importance of these developmental relationships. Second, she shared the experiences she has had in her own career about how important these relationships were for her professionally. Third, she told the group members to do whatever they wanted with this information (including doing nothing). The results? The group members embraced this concept and did some preliminary reading on the power of relationship building to enhance their own development. They shared these readings with each other. Next, they took the following actions:

1. They brainstormed a list of those leaders within the organization who were both successful and key relationship-builders;

2. Each group member then contacted one of these individuals and requested a meeting during which they would be interviewed about their views on what made them successful and, if both agreed, the leader would consider being a potential informal mentor.

Another example is a customer service manager who had gone through a formal 360-degree process in which he received anonymous quantitative and qualitative feedback on his effectiveness as a leader. This was followed by a one-hour developmental session with a leadership coach. This manager found some insights about what he needed to do to enhance his career and validation confirming what he was already doing. However, the process ended there because there were only enough funds to pay for the 360-degree assessment and one hour with the developmental coach.

The leader then took the initiative and looked for a mentor in his organization whom he perceived was gifted at what he needed to improve—delegation. Not just delegation in a generic sense, but someone who was talented at delegating truly important, meaningful work to others. He found such a person and asked her to coach him in this area (to which she agreed). Three things happened:

1. The manager discovered that he actually learned from this process and became much better at delegating important work to his team.

2. The coach learned so much from this process that she offered to be a coach to others in the organization.

3. The manager himself became a coach to others in the organization.

In a nutshell, leadership begets leadership and relationship building can expand exponentially in organizations.

[40]

Encourage Service in the Community

INVOLVEMENT IN the community is an important element of leadership. Serving on a board or advisory committee will develop leadership in a number of ways. First, the person involved will need to practice influence, which is at the heart of leadership. Likewise, the experience will challenge the individual to quickly acclimate to the inner workings of a new organization, a variety of personalities, and even new roles. For instance, challenging individuals to work outside the scope of their "work" role can be stimulating and highly developmental. After all, boards are involved in many aspects of the organization—personnel, strategic planning, development/fund-raising, performance monitoring, and stakeholder engagement.

For those of you who work with younger, emerging leaders who may not be ready to serve at the board level, there are a number of opportunities in your community to get involved in organizations such as Toastmasters, Inc., Kiwanis, Rotary, or other emerging-leadership programs that target younger professionals.

We worked in one organization that encouraged its members to serve on various boards throughout the community. Doing so not only created positive community relations, but it built relationships, increased knowledge, and complemented the good work being done in the community. In another organization, part of everyone's performance review included being assessed on their contributions to the community. Individuals were encouraged to play as small or large a part as they wanted—as long as they were contributing to a social entity other than the work organization. This process was given validity by aligning it with the performance review process.

[41]

Get Out in the Field

L EADERS MUST HAVE an awareness of their customer's or client's experience. Whether these individuals are internal or external to the organization, it is crucial that your team have a grasp on the perspective of your key constituents. This is important for a number of reasons. First, showing an interest in the experience of your customers will stand out from the crowd. In other words, you will be perceived as going above and beyond that of other service providers. The gesture communicates an interest in the client experience that is not often prioritized. Likewise, the process will shine a light on some of the challenges or opportunities for improvement. Of course, the entire process also serves as ongoing training and development for the employee, as well.

While a simple idea in theory, much can be done with the newfound knowledge acquired via the experience. For instance, you could ask your team members to provide a report that highlights opportunities for improved service and then ask him or her to champion the process. Likewise, you could charge your employee with assembling a team to work on the problem and then ask her to present reflections to key decision makers (an offshoot of Tip #22: Establish Action Learning Projects).

A manager in a nonprofit agency invited select employees to spend a day with their clients. Beforehand, she worked with these employees to develop an observation and reflection template. They observed key predetermined criteria and then jotted notes regarding their reflections of each. Not only was the learning inspiring for each employee, great conversations occurred when these employees got together as a group and shared their learning with each other. This manager now has this as part of every employee's development process.

[42]

Coordinate an On-Boarding Process

THINK BACK for a moment about your first day of work. We hope it was memorable. We hope that your new boss welcomed you, the team made you feel at home, and your e-mail and computer were up and running and ready to go. We hope! However, in our work with organizations, we have found that the on-boarding process is often an overlooked and haphazard affair. The one-day organizational new-employee training may be a little better, but we imagine the dark rooms, PowerPoint slides, and talking heads did little to energize, excite, and acclimate you to your actual department.

Helping transition an individual to your department and your organization is an important process. First impressions are lasting impressions. We have all had internships or even started a job where the new employer seemed unprepared, disinterested, or even annoyed by the inconvenience of bringing us up to speed. What a horrible message to send to a new employee. The coordination of an on-boarding process is crucial to not only the culture of your department but to the acclimation of your new team member. So whether it is a summer intern or a full-time employee, do not take this process lightly.

Here are some thoughts for a successful on-boarding process. First, be sure all the "stuff" is taken care of. This may include, but is not limited to, business cards, computer, phone line, e-mail address, and cell phone for starters. In our opinion, the second most important item is the process of relationship building. New team members must be given the time to meet others and begin building meaningful relationships. By doing so, you are displaying your commitment to a team atmosphere. Next, be sure that you or the person in charge of the on-boarding process spends extra time to get to know the new team member and provides some of the one-on-one mentorship. Also, it is important to clearly outline expectations, standards, and even some of the departmental nuances that one needs to know to be successful. Finally, be sure that there is ongoing support, development, and coaching.

[43]

Facilitate Cross-Departmental Problem Solving

ALL TOO OFTEN, organizational issues are solved by one or two leaders who, in all likelihood, do not have to implement the decisions. This is often left to the front-line employee, which hurts motivation and does not develop leadership. Stop! Bring front-line team members along for the discussion. If you teach team members how to have these conversations with other departments, they will be more likely to solve issues on their own in the future. This develops an employee's leadership capacity for problem solving outside his or her own arena.

Contact the director of the other department and request a brainstorming meeting. This should not be confrontational in nature—simply a meeting to help alleviate stress on both ends (recall Tip #4: Model Effective Confrontation). If the two directors and a few front-line team members are part of the solution, it is more likely that the results will stick. It also gets the team members to think like leaders. At the beginning, you and the other department leader could state the problem and turn it over to the team members to solve among themselves. This action fosters communication among different levels of the organization. Try this idea and you will be amazed at how well it can work. Your role in this approach is to facilitate. The front-line team members' challenge is to problem solve—let them learn firsthand how difficult (and rewarding) this process can be.

If you're a leader with several layers of management reporting to you, walk your talk. Executives are often the worst offenders of problem solving outside their spheres of influence. One example of this can been seen in the myriad times we have attended executive team

meetings. Here's the typical scenario. Let's say there's a marketing issue. It may be discussed on the executive team, but peripherally.
What often happens is that, after a brief discussion, the problem is
turned over to the marketing leader for further analysis "up and
down" her chain of command. We're not saying that this is ineffective.
We are saying that more time must be spent within the executive
team to get a sense of the divergent views from a variety of disciplines.
Then it could be taken to others within the marketing system for further analysis. Or, if the analysis is made within the marketing area,
the executive can then bring it to the table with the full executive
team for a robust discussion of potential considerations that would
be worth the marketing team's attention.

These strategies help potential leaders understand that leadership
is about understanding the needs of the organization from diverse
perspectives. One hallmark of a good leader is the ability to transcend
multiple viewpoints—this tip is a first step in being exposed to these
perspectives.

[44]

Create Teachers and *Leaders*

Teaching is the highest form of learning. Likewise, great leaders are great teachers. Over the years, we have discovered that the person who teaches a course often learns the most. There are individuals in your organization who teach courses in local community colleges or continuing education courses in the community. A great way to develop those around you is to have them teach within your organization. Maybe it is a course or a roundtable on your department and its services. Maybe it is an informational seminar for internal constituents so they can better understand how your department functions. It could even be a course for customers.

Think about those daily issues that bother you and those around you. Which of these issues could be cut off at the pass with a little education of key stakeholders? Brainstorm these issues with your team and determine how each can be addressed through education. Then ask one or two of your team members to take on the problem and implement a solution. This way, you are developing your team and assisting your department in communicating its message.

A variation of this approach is a strategy in which management training is cofacilitated by a training/human resource specialist and an operations manager. These "nontraining managers" are taught in the art and science of presentation and facilitation skills. The results can be outstanding. In one scenario we learned about, managers who attended the "train the trainer" sessions placed much more credibility in the program than when it was facilitated by a training specialist alone. More important, participants appeared more attentive than when the session was facilitated by only the training professional. The program ended up nearly "standing room only" for most of the sessions—including those that were five-day residential sessions requiring an extensive time commitment. Participants wanted and valued hearing the views of operations leaders. And finally, a serendipitous discovery was made . . . those nontraining specialists (e.g., the operations leaders) who cofacilitated the sessions noted that they became much more adept not only at coaching and facilitating but also at implementing what they taught.

[45]

Give Out the Monumental Assignment

THE MONUMENTAL ASSIGNMENT begins with a simple question: What crucial projects have failed in recent years? Yes, failed. Make a quick list of these and now think about whom you could ask to be the next in line to give it a go. In fact, if you are looking for a great way to really challenge someone, assign them an account, an initiative, or some other project that simply did not work the last time it was attempted. Packaged in this simple concept can be a number of opportunities for growth and development. In fact, it can include any of the tips we have been writing about in one big developmental assignment. After all, there is risk of failure in oftentimes a visible way. Of course, there needs to be some probability that the task actually can be accomplished, but by challenging high-potential employees in this manner, you will gain a glimpse into what they are really made of. Can they solve problems creatively? Handle stressful systems? Navigate organizational politics? Work across departments or industries? Build and lead a team? Influence others? Sell an idea or concept? Manage a project?

We understand that some of you may hesitate to set someone up for failure or even the *potential* for failure. However, when chosen wisely, these opportunities can be an opportunity for a team member to shine and your organization to take a risk in a healthy manner. Likewise, projects that have failed in the past may serve as an opportunity to learn from past mistakes and truly impact the organization in a positive manner. Choose these opportunities wisely (and with caution) and be sure to support those involved all along the way.

We heard from one manager who reported very positive results using this strategy. What he did was have employees report periodically regarding one failure (or something that did not proceed in an anticipated, positive way). Not only did he encourage this, but he made room for this at every team meeting by carving out five minutes for this process. While at first people were reluctant to do this, they quickly learned the power of failure. What appeared to encourage this more than anything was not only the five minutes within the ninety-minute weekly meetings, but also the fact that the manager himself modeled this by talking about his own failures. And it's not just the failure that is key—it's the retrospective analysis in which one addresses what they might do differently next time. Of course, others may chime in with additional ideas to help out the individual. And one serendipitous finding here was that people sometimes discovered that they did not fail as much as they thought—either because of the learning that occurred in this process or because others pointed out some of the positive results they might have overlooked.

Development Through Feedback

[46]

Create a Culture of Feedback

LEADERS IN organizations and communities often have a difficult time providing others with feedback in a constructive way. For many, it takes only a moment to recall an inappropriate remark made in the spirit of trying to be helpful—whether delivered as a shout, as gossip, or in a condescending manner. Such divisive behavior among coworkers and supervisors and their direct reports can linger for years and can inhibit productivity and a true sense of "team." It all comes down to supportive communication. If you have an environment with healthy communication, it is much more likely to be productive. Do your coworkers a favor: Create an environment in which team members have an opportunity to provide one another (and you) with feedback in a healthy and productive manner. Creating this culture will pay off tenfold. Otherwise, you may end up with a "toxic culture" and need to find more profound systems interventions, as Kusy and Holloway[24] found in their research on toxic personalities.

As a team, develop healthy ground rules surrounding the communication process. After all, disagreement in a team is to be expected, but how you disagree is critical to being a constructive critic. As with everything else in this book, it starts with you. If you provide feedback in a supportive manner, then others around you will have a greater tendency to do the same. If you are willing to accept constructive criticism, then it is likely that others around you will follow suit. If you are willing to put in the effort to create an environment of open communication, others may follow your lead.

Try the following strategy for providing feedback to another individual, whether it is positive or negative. We call it the ID—GAP model:

BOX 6. THE ID—GAP MODEL

► Identify the behavior you would like to comment on.

► Describe the behavior in specific and concrete terms.

► Give feedback as to how this behavior affects you—positively or negatively. Pause and give the person an opportunity to respond.

► Assess what either you or the other person might do differently. Negotiate these differences.

► Plan how both of you will follow up.

Considering the many clients, coworkers, and/or supervisors with whom we have worked over the years, this is an area that appears to be one of the most troublesome for leaders—how to manage the performance of others. We can easily count a dozen or so of our clients within the past six months who have had this challenge. They flounder because, sometimes, they just don't know how to have difficult conversations or provide feedback to others. One leader told us that having this kind of a template helped her initiate the process and provided a game plan for her team. Please note that it certainly doesn't have to be our model. However, we have found that it needs to be *some* model that provides a road map to foster the feedback process.

[47]

Set Aside Time for Self-Evaluation

W E ALL KNOW people who have no clue as to how they "come off" to others around them. Self-evaluations are one way to develop leadership capacity on an ongoing basis. These do not need to be cumbersome processes. For instance, it may be two simple questions, such as "What are you doing well in our department?" and "Where could you improve?" By helping your team members reflect on their work, you develop their awareness, which, in turn, develops your "bench strength."

Of course, you will run into some people who have no idea that they need to improve, but you still need to start the conversation at some point. This tool is an opportunity to begin chipping away and helping team members see another point of view. These self-evaluations should be completed a couple of times a year. You might even ask your team to put their thoughts on paper; this may serve as another form of reflection or link to their development plan (see Tip #36: Foster Growth Through Personal Development Plans). If you would like to take this concept to the next level, ask those around you to answer the same questions for *you*, as well; doing so will allow you an opportunity for honest feedback and may help you understand how you can better work with each individual on your team. Moreover you will be modeling the way (Tip #2). A huge mistake would be to assume that one management style fits all. This is not the case.

[48]

Provide Development Through Assessment

U SE OF ASSESSMENT TOOLS is another way to develop those on your team. Of course, one can debate the effectiveness of one tool versus another and, at times, your team members will complain of their frustrations with them—"I hate these things" or "They never capture me" or "I don't know how to answer . . . It depends on the situation." However, assessment tools can be a great way of helping people become more aware of their work styles, personalities, temperaments, and ways of communicating.

Assessments help people become more self-aware. Often, an individual in an organization or in the community at large will be trained in a number of these tools. A few to consider include:

- ► Emotional-Social Competency Inventory (ESCI)
- ► Multifactor Leadership Questionnaire (MLQ)
- ► The Yale Assessment of Thinking
- ► The Myers-Briggs Type Indicator (MBTI)
- ► The Thomas-Kilman Conflict Mode Instrument
- ► Kolb's Learning Style Inventory (LSI)
- ► StrengthsFinder
- ► Keirsey Temperament Sorter

Note that some of these tools require a certified administrator. However, one option is to use trained facilitators for the assessment piece and initial facilitation. Then, you can do the follow-up by scheduling regular meetings when you and the team review progress and application on the job. Be sure to have people coach one another—you do not have to do all the coaching. Remember, you want to develop the leadership capacity of your team.

As with all these tips, get involved and approach the learning in a positive manner—learning does not have to be an activity conducted in dark rooms with PowerPoint slides.

[49]

Ask the Tough Questions

PEOPLE GROW when they are challenged to think and act in new and different ways. What all of us do on a day-to-day basis gets us to where we are. So, if we want to go somewhere new, we need to incorporate innovative ways of thinking and behaving. Asking the tough questions can assist in this process. Tough questions about the status of team cohesion, team decisions, and departmental challenges will take your team to the next level. Meaningful conversations will help your team accept and work through differing perspectives. High-functioning teams can disagree and still produce excellent products and results. They can disagree and still care about each other. Members of high-functioning teams will challenge each other to think differently. As the leader, you have a responsibility to create this environment.

Begin with the question "How can we take this team to the next level?" The first few times you ask this question, you will probably get blank stares (this is either because they may not trust you or because they are not used to having these types of conversations). Keep chipping away slowly and steadfastly and, we predict, eventually they will talk and take ownership.

If the team needs some help determining what to talk about, we suggest you discuss work styles and perceived drawbacks and strengths, and ask others to help aid in the team's development. On a consistent basis, revisit the conversation and simply start the discussion with "So how are we doing?" You will be amazed at the dialogue these questions can spark, many times cutting off a potential issue before it is elevated into a larger one. In addition, more often than not, team members share with the group areas for improvement before anyone else had to say it. Box 8 provides examples of some tough questions for leaders to consider.

BOX 7. THE TOUGH QUESTIONS

▶ What are some obstacles affecting this team?

▶ What are opportunities we could take advantage of that we have been largely ignoring?

▶ Where can you take greater ownership on this team?

▶ Where have you let this team down?

▶ Compared to other teams with which you are familiar, how are we doing?

▶ When was the last time you complimented the team or one of its members?

▶ How open are you to giving direct feedback to team members?

[50]

Capture the Learning from Hardships and Failure

HARDSHIPS ARE developmental experiences that are not planned for. In fact, they are, quite often, not pleasant for the individual experiencing the hardship. Regarding hardships, Russ Moxley of the Center for Creative Leadership suggests, "Hardships are important to the development of well-rounded leaders. Learning is not random. Specific experiences teach specific lessons, and hardships offer lessons not attainable elsewhere."[25]

The Center for Creative Leadership has identified five types of organizationally related hardships and the lessons each may teach an individual. These include: business mistakes and failures, career setbacks, personal trauma, problem employees, and downsizing.[26] It is possible that individuals may experience one or all of these hardships and never learn from them. Although not an exhaustive list, three elements may help your team members learn and grow from hardships. These include critical reflection, supportive environment/relationships, and flexibility. Understanding why the hardship has happened and what is needed to move on are components of critical reflection in this context. Supportive relationships can help individuals better understand and make meaning of the hardships they endured. A strong network of friends and family can help them pick up the pieces and reflect on the events that led to the hardship. In addition, a support network can help keep the hardship in perspective. And finally, flexibility is needed to help individuals use a wide array of internal and external resources to react appropriately and effectively.

People are confronted with work-related hardships every day. Our point is that this concept needs to be a part of the collective conversation of leadership development so that learning moments associated with these events can be captured and capitalized upon. Knowing that you and the people around you face hardships better helps you and your team plan for them in your department or organization. No one can predict a tornado, but when one comes, it is best to be prepared.

So set up an environment where people feel comfortable sharing selected hardships. There's a twofold purpose for this. It is often cathartic in the sense that when people talk about an issue publicly there's a greater probability that they will work through it more quickly than had they said nothing. Second, we have discovered that, by sharing hardships with others, there is greater realization that one is not alone in the process. Others may have been through similar circumstances. This can prompt an invaluable discussion on ways to deal with the hardship—probably the most important dimension of the process.

In the book *Breaking the Code of Silence*, the authors found that the most successful leaders have addressed their devastating errors first by talking about them and then having a specific recovery plan for any of the seven common mistakes a leader has made.[27] The fact that the leaders talked about these serious blunders in such an intense and open way was validated by the fact that 100 percent of the leaders the authors interviewed gave them permission to use their quotes in the book. Yes, 100 percent. So, it may go without saying—but we would like to emphasize this outstanding method of developing the leadership capacity of others—establish an environment in which discussion of hardships is encouraged and follow with potential ways to deal with them.

The point is to model this for others and encourage others to follow suit. When leaders walk their talk, others are likely to do the same. So, when leaders learn from hardships, share their experiences with others, and coach others *through* these experiences, true leadership capacity is developed.

Conclusion

DEVELOPING LEADERSHIP CAPACITY in others is important and vital work. As we said, leaders are, in part, responsible for creating the culture of their departments. Leaders are no longer "worker bees," per se, but they facilitate the work of those individuals on the front line. *Facilitate* is an important word. Take a quick look at dictionary.com and you will find that *facilitate* means "to make easy or easier." Another definition is "to increase the likelihood, strength, or effectiveness of (as behavior or a response)." A number of management texts prescribe that the four primary functions of a manager are to "plan, lead, organize, and control." To us, this sounds a little archaic—in fact, cobwebs come to mind. Not that these words are inherently wrong, but we could place the word *facilitate* in front of each.

The days of the manager, vice president, or CEO knowing everything about the business are over; business is just too complex. As a result, members at each level of management must become masters at facilitating processes and tasks at all levels of the organization. They have to work with others to obtain optimal results because going it alone simply does not match the current business environment. All of us must have the ability to "facilitate" planning, leading, organizing, and controlling. In our experience, facilitation does not come to many managers naturally and, in some cases, it is not their fault that they haven't learned this. After all, it has not been part of the dominant paradigm of management in business.

Likewise, the days of lavish training budgets and off-site facilities are fewer and farther between. Tuition reimbursement and travel budgets are being cut. Much of the training in Fortune 500 corporations has moved to an e-learning format. This is fine, and certainly has its place, but few would disagree that having a human being as a coach and mentor is a much more fulfilling and rewarding experience.

So, as the pace of organizational life continues to increase and our scope increases to a global community, we truly wonder where employees will gain the skills they need to be successful. The answer, in part, is that *you* will need to facilitate the development of your people. Yes, one more task added to an already full plate, but we believe that if done well, time, money, and resources can be saved, individuals will have a better developmental experience, and we will *truly* be building leadership capacity in our people. Hopefully, as many of the tips in this book suggest, it is aligned with the strategic priorities of your department and the organization.

Here's a favorite quote of ours that applies to this discussion: "Every system is perfectly designed for the results it gets." Think about this quote for a few moments. The system of customer service at Nordstrom is different from that of K-mart. The system of customer service is different at the Ritz Carlton than at the Days Inn. Systems are all around us. We each have a system of how we manage our money, keep our house, and parent our children. Some systems yield great results, and others . . . not so good. In fact, your department has a system of leadership development. We would guess that, for some readers, the "system" may be that there isn't one, and for others, it may be quite robust and advanced.

Regardless, if you would like to get somewhere new, the system needs to be tweaked. After all, we know the results of the current system. You have gotten this far in the book because you would like to try something new. So let's get to work at "facilitating" the development of a new system that will provide your team members with the knowledge, skills, and abilities to lead your organization more effectively. To get you started, we suggest completing The Leadership Development 50 (LD50 Snapshot).

The LD50 Snapshot

INSTRUCTIONS: This quick and easy assessment is designed to provide you with a snapshot of your *current* leadership development system. Read each tip and circle the number that corresponds with the current level of success you are having with the suggestion. If the tip does not exist in your culture, simply write in NAF for "Not a Fit" or OPP for "Opportunity." Once you have completed the assessment, step back and evaluate your system by completing the following steps:

- ▶ Of the tips that do exist, how many are working at high levels? Place a check next to these.

- ▶ Of the tips that do not exist, which could be implemented with relative ease? Place a box around these.

- ▶ Of the tips you have given a box, which two best align with your current culture and can be implemented with relative ease? Place a star next to these.

- ▶ Finally, read through the list and identify one tip that aligns with the needs of individual members of your team. Place their names next to these.

Once you have completed this exercise, we suggest you consult with your staff, peers, and/or other colleagues for corroboration that your selection is one that is most critical. Based on that feedback, you may find some other tips that are in need of greater attention. Involve others as you feel appropriate.

Another approach is to give this instrument to direct reports, colleagues, and/or peers and have them engage in this activity. Then, compare their feedback with your own assessment. If there are points of disagreement, these are opportunities ripe for discussion. All in all, use your judgment as to how you want to proceed. But whatever you develop, communicate with your staff. Remember, to be a leader is to teach and facilitate—and what better way to do this than to model the learning and action process.

Finally, remember that developing leadership capacity is not a one-time event. Revisit this activity periodically and adjust your sails accordingly. Time is not the only variable, though. As you bring new people into your organization, use this assessment and matrix system to steer the course in successful and innovative ways. With this as a backdrop, you'll be a leader who truly builds leadership capacity in others and who leads with vision and innovation.

Current Rating of Success:

Very Low	Low	Neutral	High	Very High
1	2	3	4	5

_____ 1. Clarify Team Expectations

_____ 2. Model the Way

_____ 3. Recognize and Reward Achievement

_____ 4. Model Effective Confrontation

_____ 5. Provide Challenge *and* Support

_____ 6. Keep the Troops in the Loop

_____ 7. Check in with a Thought of the Day

_____ 8. Realize Your Team Is *Your* Customer

_____ 9. Use the Pygmalion Effect

_____ 10. Coach for Performance

_____ 11. Facilitate a Culture of Accountability

_____ 12. Tap into Their Passion, Unleash the Energy

_____ 13. Hold Standing One-on-Ones

_____ 14. Help Make *Their* Vision a Reality

_____ 15. Solidify Their Learning

_____ 16. Stretch Your Team. Always

_____ 17. Switch It Up

_____ 18. Have *Them* Lead the Team

_____ 19. Create Great Communicators

_____ 20. Grow Their Roles

_____ 21. Let Them Answer the "How"

_____ 22. Establish Action Learning Projects

_____ 23. Design a Department Retreat

_____ 24. Implement an Operating Calendar

_____ 25. Create a Culture of Benchmarking

_____ 26. Foster Critical Reflection

_____ 27. Host a Book/Article Club

_____ 28. Foster a Friendly Debate

_____ 29. Create an Organizational FAQ

_____ 30. Conduct a *Quick* Case Study

_____ 31. Bring in Support

_____ 32. Remain Focused on the Solutions, *Not* the Barriers

_____ 33. Conduct After-Action Reviews

_____ 34. Help Diagnose the Challenge—Technical or Adaptive?

_____ 35. Transfer *School* Work Back to *Your* Work

_____ 36. Foster Growth Through Personal Development Plans

_____ 37. Capture and Share the Learning

_____ 38. Develop Emotional Intelligence

_____ 39. Facilitate Developmental Relationships

_____ 40. Encourage Service in the Community

_____ 41. Get Out in the Field

_____ 42. Coordinate an On-Boarding Process

_____ 43. Facilitate Cross-Departmental Problem Solving

_____ 44. Create Teachers *and* Leaders

_____ 45. Give Out the Monumental Assignment

_____ 46. Create a Culture of Feedback

_____ 47. Set Aside Time for Self-Evaluation

_____ 48. Provide Development Through Assessment

_____ 49. Ask the Tough Questions

_____ 50. Capture the Learning from Hardships and Failure

Notes

1. Bernard Bass, *Bass and Stogdill's Handbook of Leadership: Theory, Research and Managerial Application* (3rd edition) (New York: The Free Press, 1990), 854.
2. A. A. Huczynski and J. W. Lewis, "An Empirical Study into the Learning Transfer Process in Management Training," *Journal of Management Studies* 17 (1980): 227–240.
3. J. C. Norcross, A. C. Ratzkin, and D. Payne, "Ringing in the New Year: The Change Process and Reported Outcomes of Resolutions," *Addictive Behaviors,* 14 (1989): 205–212.
4. L. N. Essex and M. E. Kusy, *Manager's Desktop Consultant: Just-in-Time Solutions to the Top People Problems That Keep You Up at Night* (Mountain View, CA: Davies-Black Publishing, 2007).
5. Jay Conger, *Learning to Lead: The Art of Transforming Managers into Leaders* (San Francisco, CA: Jossey-Bass, 1992).
6. D. A. Whetten and K. S. Cameron, *Developing Management Skills* (8th edition) (Upper Saddle River, New Jersey: Prentice Hall, 2010).
7. Marcus Buckingham and Curt Coffman, *First Break All the Rules: What the World's Greatest Managers Do Differently* (New York: Simon & Schuster, 1999).
8. Bruce J. Avolio and Fred Luthans, *The High Impact Leader* (New York: McGraw Hill, 2006).
9. Mitchell Kusy and Elizabeth Holloway, *Toxic Workplace: Managing Toxic Personalities and Their Systems of Power* (San Francisco, CA: Jossey-Bass, 2009).
10. K. Kelloway, J. Barling, E. Kelley, J. Comtois, and B. Gatien, "Remote Transformational Leadership," *Leadership and Organization Development Journal* 24 (2003): 163–171.
11. Bernard Bass, *Leadership and Performance Beyond Expectations* (New York: The Free Press, 1985), 71.
12. Buckingham and Coffman.

13. Bernard Bass and Bruce Avolio, *Improving Organization Effectiveness Through Transformational Leadership* (Thousand Oaks, CA: Sage, 1994).

14. B. Clarke and R. Crossland, *The Leader's Voice: How Your Communication Can Inspire Action and Get Results!* (New York: Select Books, 2002), 6.

15. M. W. McCall, M. M. Lombardo, and A. M. Morrison, *The Lessons of Experience: How Successful Executives Develop on the Job* (Lexington, MA: Lexington Books, 1988).

16. D. Giber, L. Carter, and M. Goldsmith, *Linkage Inc.'s Best Practices in Leadership Development Handbook* (San Francisco, CA: Jossey-Bass, 2000).

17. Jack Mezirow and Associates, *Learning as Transformation: Critical Perspectives on a Theory in Progress* (San Francisco, CA: Jossey-Bess, 2000).

18. Stephen Brookfield, *Understanding and Facilitating Adult Learning* (San Francisco, CA: Jossey-Bass, 1986).

19. Bruce Avolio, *Leadership Development in Balance: Made/Born* (Mahwah, NJ: Lawrence Earlbaum Associates, 2005).

20. Marcy Shankman and Scott Allen, *Emotionally Intelligent Leadership: A Guide for College Students* (San Francisco, CA: Jossey-Bass, 2008), 12.

21. Ronald Heifetz and Martin Linsky, *Leadership on the Line: Staying Alive Through the Dangers of Leading* (Cambridge, MA: Harvard Business Press, 2002), 51.

22. Daniel Goleman, *Emotional Intelligence: Why It Can Matter More Than IQ* (New York: Bantam Books, 1995).

23. Giber, Carter, and Goldsmith.

24. Mitchell Kusy and Elizabeth Holloway, *Toxic Workplace: Managing Toxic Personalities and Their Systems of Power* (San Francisco, CA: Jossey-Bass, 2009).

25. R. Moxley and P. O'Conner-Wilson, *The Center for Creative Leadership Handbook of Leadership Development*, eds. C. McCauley, R. Moxley, and E. Van Velsor (San Francisco, CA: Jossey-Bass, 1998).

26. Ibid.

27. M. Kusy and L. Essex, *Breaking the Code of Silence: Prominent Leaders Reveal How They Rebounded from Seven Critical Mistakes* (Lanham, MD: Taylor Trade Publishing, 2005).

Index

About the Authors

Scott J. Allen, Ph.D., is an assistant professor of management at John Carroll University, where he teaches courses in leadership and management skills. Scott is also the coauthor of *Emotionally Intelligent Leadership: A Guide for College Students* (Jossey-Bass) and the corresponding suite of resources (Workbook and Facilitation and Activity Guide). In addition, Scott has articles published in the *Journal of Leadership Educators, Journal of Leadership Studies, Advances in Developing Human Resources, Leadership Review, The International Leadership Journal, The OD Journal, SAM Advanced Management Journal,* and *Leadership Excellence.* Along with writing and speaking, Scott blogs (www.weeklyleader.net), consults, facilitates workshops, and leads retreats across industries. He resides in Chagrin Falls, Ohio, with his wife, Jessica, and three children—Will, Kate, and Emily.

Dr. Mitchell Kusy (Mitch) has had twenty-five years' experience in leadership and organization development (OD). A Registered OD Consultant, he is a full professor in the Ph.D. Program, Leadership & Change, Antioch University, and a distinguished visiting professor at the University of Auckland, New Zealand. Internationally, he has consulted in more than fifteen countries and recently received the international honor of being selected a Fulbright Scholar in international organization development. In 1998, he received the prestigious Minnesota Organization Development Practitioner of the Year award.

Previous to his position at Antioch University, Mitch was a full professor in the master's and doctoral program in organization development at the University of St. Thomas, Minneapolis, where he taught for seventeen years. Before entering academia, Mitch worked in industry and directed the leadership development area at American Express

Financial Advisors; before that, he managed organization development and employee relations for Health Partners, Inc.

His latest book is coauthored with Dr. Elizabeth Holloway and is entitled *Toxic Workplace! Managing Toxic Personalities and Their Systems of Power.* It is based on their research study on the specific strategies leaders should employ to mitigate the effects of toxic personalities at work. His publication record consists of hundreds of articles and the following books coauthored with Dr. Louellen Essex: *Manager's Desktop Consultant: Just-in-Time Solutions to the Top People Problems That Keep You Up at Night* (Davies-Black Publishing); *Fast Forward Leadership: How to Exchange Outmoded Practices for Forward-Looking Leadership Today* (Financial Times-Prentice Hall); and *Breaking the Code of Silence: Prominent Leaders Reveal How They Rebounded from Seven Critical Mistakes* (Taylor Trade Publishing/ Rowman & Littlefield Publishing Group).